The
'FOB'S KID'
Syndrome

The
'FOB'S KID'
Syndrome

Vulcan Bombers in Action
By Crew Chief Barry Goodwin

Airlife
England

Copyright © 2001 Barry Goodwin

First published in the UK in 2001
by Airlife Publishing Ltd

British Library Cataloguing-in-Publication Data
A catalogue record for this book
is available from the British Library

ISBN 1 84037 266 4

Typeset by Phoenix Typesetting, Ilkley, West Yorkshire
Printed in England by St Edmundsbury Press Ltd., Bury St Edmunds, Suffolk.

Airlife Publishing Ltd

101 Longden Road, Shrewsbury, SY3 9EB England.
E-mail: airlife@airlifebooks.com
Website:www.airlifebooks.com

DEDICATION

This book is dedicated to Mike Francis, whose efforts in the campaign to keep Vulcan XH558 flying were my inspiration. He kept my nose to the grindstone, and badgered me to complete this book when my will appeared to falter.

ACKNOWLEDGEMENTS

My thanks for the photographs supplied by Mike Francis and Steve Mills.

XM655 sits on ORP 1 at RAF Finningley. It is now a 'live' aircraft at Wellsbourne Mountford.

PREFACE

The acronym 'FOB'S KID' or 'Fed On Bull Shit and Kept In the Dark' was an expression that circulated amongst the ground crew, who looked after the mighty Vulcan bomber force, and the aircrew that flew them. This was during those uncertain days after the country's nuclear deterrent capability had been passed to the submarines of the Royal Navy.

Within the Royal Air Force, there was an atmosphere of forced impotence prevailing as the bombers took on their newer role of low-level interdiction and the expression, symbolised by 'FOB'S KID', describes exactly how the men sometimes felt. There was a continual succession of alert and dispersal exercises, and departures at a moment's notice for destinations unknown – and for indeterminate periods of time. This led at one point to the adoption of a mushroom symbol as an unofficial emblem. This did, of course, have wider nuclear connotations, also as a badge of convenience. It makes a fitting title for this book which tries to capture the atmosphere of the operation of the 'V' force in those trying times through the eyes of a Crew Chief.

As well as being general dogsbody, the Crew Chief was the inventory holder of 'his' Vulcan – everything that was contained within the airframe, indeed the airframe itself, was on his charge. He was responsible for the maintenance, servicing and repair of his Bomber, and in the old days, would stay with it through thick and thin.

He was trained in engines, airframes, electrics, and instruments, with a smattering of radio thrown in for good measure. The training course was a year long and, for airframe fitters, began with an engines course at St Athan in South Wales. For engine fitters, the first course was in Airframes. The electronics phase was then carried out at Newton, near to Nottingham, with the final Vulcan airframe phase at Finningley. Postings were then meted out to one of the V-bomber force stations throughout the UK.

A probationary period of about six months was required alongside an experienced Crew Chief before a new Chief became 'operational' and then he was on his own.

'The job' was very demanding, and was held responsible for the break up of many marriages, as the 'other woman', the Vulcan, always seemed to have precedence in the life of its Crew Chief.

The Battle of Britain memorial flight flies over Vulcan XM655 whilst parked on the ORP at an air display.

CONTENTS

The author prepares to see off XM655 at RAF Finningley for a V.I.P.
demonstration scramble.

CHAPTER 1

SCRAMBLE

The Crew Chief shivered in the thin chill wind as it filtered down the runway and across the concrete of the ORP (Operational Readiness Platform) where he stood. Dawn was breaking over the bleak airfield at Waddington in Lincolnshire as the breath of the Chief and his handling crew clouded briefly in the cold air, to be swirled across the airfield, along with the diesel exhaust fumes from the power set connected to their slumbering metal monster.

It had been a long hard night, as nights always were on QRA (Quick Reaction Alert) duty. Limbs ached and eyes watered, whilst cold feet were stamped in vain on the unyielding concrete surface in attempts to restore life to cold and numbed toes. Hands were thrust tightly under armpits, attempting to ease warmth and a semblance of feeling into lifeless fingers again.

For nearly an hour, the incessant whine of the 'Telebrief', the land-line connecting the aircraft intercom system to Headquarters Strike Command at High Wycombe, had permeated their eardrums. Gradually this became increasingly soporific as they sheltered under the massive structure of XM655, the Vulcan Bomber that towered above them on ORP1, imparting a feeling of remoteness which detached them from the seeming gravity of the situation. Casting a glance along the length of the ORP, they could make out the other groups of Crew Chiefs and handlers manning their aircraft, XM648 and ORP2, XM608 on ORP3 and XM657 occupying ORP4, where their situations appeared about the same – cold, bored, and bleary eyed.

The wind was channelled at an increased speed where they stood due to the perfect aerofoil shape of the aircraft undersurface. This served to increase their discomfort as they continued to wait for what seemed to be an interminable period. It seemed that the long-anticipated command to launch the mighty delta-winged bomber, together with its three sinister companions, along the runway and into the boundless sky would never come.

It was the beginning of January 1971, in the middle of the 'cold war', and in June 1969 the RAF had given over its nuclear capability to the Royal Navy. By the end of 1970, the Vulcans had been refinished in glossy polyurethane paint and even the 'Blue Steel' stand-off weapon had been given up and reduced to scrap metal. The RAF's task was now primarily to deliver 'iron' bombs, usually retarded one-thousand pounders. Exercises were still carried out with simulated nuclear weapons, or 'training weapons', to hone the crews and procedures, and to create a back-up force for the Polaris missiles should anything be required of them.

The Chief mused that this current exercise was different to others he had known since completing his ASC training at the latter end of 1969, as there had been several changes to normal procedure, but then the easiest course was just to accept these. He had learned over the years, many of these on active service (service in war zones) of one form or another, that it never paid to question such procedures too closely. This was always the simpler solution and allowed the more mundane tasks of normal operation to be carried out with their usual proficiency. These tasks were purely routine, such as towing the first

Vehicle sticker issued by
44 Squadron.

44 Squadron badge

The badge of 50 Squadron.

The flying suit patch of
101 Squadron.

The badge of 101 Squadron.

of the armed aircraft to the Operational Readiness Platform, and carrying out both the before-flight, and Crew-Chief-acceptance checks.

He was also aware that morale in the V-Force tended to be rather low at this time, as centralised servicing was in operation. This meant that the servicing personnel were in a central pool and the normally wonderful spirit that prevailed with autonomous squadron operation was missing for them entirely. Aircraft were also in a pool, and the only squadron identity was for the aircrew, being split between 101, 50 and 44 Squadrons. Squadron bonds between aircraft and aircrew did begin to creep in when crews took to adorning an aircraft selected for a particular task such as a 'lone ranger' with their squadron identity, in the form of a stick-on badge on the crew entrance door. This had no official blessing and did not in any way indicate that aircraft had been officially allocated to squadrons. Aircrew morale was a little higher than it had been earlier, in 1965, when the aircrews of No. 1 Group attended a dining-in night at RAF Waddington. After suitably priming themselves at local hostelries before the event, they aired their grievances and vented their feelings in no uncertain manner, ensuring that the famous '1 Gp Dining-In Night' entered documented history. Every officer in the entire V-Force received a bill for resultant damage after this event – irrespective of whether he had attended or not!

The 'Lineys', as the groundcrew that operated the Vulcans were known, existed in conditions of some squalor at their workplaces on the airfield, inhabiting tents that had been erected at dispersal for them to use as crew rooms. These were cold and muddy during the winter, hot and smelly in the summer, and many complaints were levied. Duckboards were laid as flooring, but these simply sank into the mud when it rained. They became known as 'Pigs' to the rest of the station, and even adopted a cloth Pig Badge that every 'Liney' wore with pride. Even the Crew Chiefs wore it on their flying suits. The wording PIG was interpreted under the emblem as 'Pride, Integrity and Guts'. It was this self publicity that eventually stirred the powers-that-be into action and, after inspection by the new station commander and his entourage of wing commanders, better accommodation was eventually afforded for the Lineys in the dispersal outbuildings. It was also the beginning of the end for centralised servicing, which was phased out around the middle of 1972. Aircraft then adopted their own squadron identity, sporting the intermeshed '44' of 44 Squadron, the running greyhounds of 50 Squadron, and the stylised '101' with the inlaid Castle and Lion of 101 Squadron superimposed on their fins. The Lineys were also allocated to their own squadrons and now had an identity, and wholeheartedly entered into the spirit of things – morale reached a new high, and the pig emblem disappeared for good!

Bringing his thoughts back to matters in hand, the Chief noted that fuel loads on the ORP aircraft were also heavier than usual, a full 72,380 lb. plus both bomb-bay tanks full – another 11,081 lb. That was a long 'ranger load' and a lot more than the ninety-eight percent usually tanked for a normal mission, or the twenty percent that was sometimes tanked to impress the crowds with a super-fast scramble and display. It seemed that there was something more sinister afoot here as this bomber, when airborne, was going on a very long journey.

It was also unusual, during an exercise, to generate every aircraft on the station as was happening this time. In periods of war, aircraft could go without an AAPP. This was an abbreviation for the Airborne Auxiliary Power Pack which, basically, was an on-board Rover gas turbine engine used to drive a generator, and also to supply high-volume, low-pressure air for starting the engines. The Chief was also reliably informed that the Vulcans could fly without an engine, and with all manner of other unserviceability – getting them to the target was all that mattered after all. If they could do that with success then the object of their existence had been achieved. In the ultimate

The Liney's pig badge

situation, that of war, just how they returned, to where they returned, or to what they returned, was never talked about.

Experiments were also being carried out at the time where Vulcans would fly in close support with 'Gnat' fighters off the east coast, and these would be used in exercise situations to simulate the release of enemy stand-off weapons from an incoming carrier aircraft. Fighter defences would be scrambled to meet them, usually with some modicum of success. The Chiefs would hear the stories from the aircrew when returning from such sorties, making light of it all, and usually bored out of their minds with what seemed to them to be a pointless exercise.

A sudden squeal of tyres on the concrete of the ORP nearby woke the Chief from his reverie. This heralded the arrival of a Land Rover with welcome coffee that was taken thankfully by the eager ground-crew. This was only to find that numbed lips had not sensed the extreme temperature of the hot, sweet, 'NATO standard' liquid, and scalded tongues, accompanied by much cursing, were the inevitable result.

The Crew Chief turned to remonstrate, unreasonably perhaps, with the driver but was cut short by a half-expected yet attention-grabbing and staccato voice of command in his earphones through the Telebrief: 'Attention, attention, this is the Bomber Controller – for Waddington, Scampton, and Cottesmore wings – maintain readiness state zero-five – I repeat, Waddington, Scampton, and Cottesmore wings – maintain readiness state zero-five – Bomber Controller out.'

'Ahhh . . . shit!' retorted the unidentified voice of a crew member over the whine of the Telebrief, 'If we've still got to hang around like this for much longer we may as well open the soup and break out the sandwiches'.

'No, not now, save it 'til later – we may need it more then. We're sure to go soon, we've been crewed in for a long time now!' cautioned another voice which the Chief assumed to be that of the captain. Eventually, with a few more disgruntled utterances, the crew quietened down, once again allowing the penetrating whine of the Telebrief to take over and numb their senses to the point of oblivion again.

'Attention, attention – this is the Bomber Controller – for Scampton and Cottesmore wings only – revert to readiness state one-five – I repeat Scampton and Cottesmore wings only – revert to readiness one-five – Bomber Controller out.'

With one accord the complaining, but seemingly resigned, voices of the aircrew piped up again.

'Oh bloody 'ell!' exclaimed one, 'What on earth are they playing at now?'

'Why are we still at zero five then?' questioned another.

'Pipe down in the back there,' came the authoritative voice of the captain, 'you know we'll either go soon or revert to one-five ourselves.'

More banter ensued until, eventually, silence reigned again and boredom began to take its toll once more.

'Just think!' remarked another detached voice suddenly, 'I passed up a night out in Lincoln tonight for this – I wonder if we'll get away in time to get to the 'Morning Star' before it closes? If we do, I'll bet I catch my bird drinking with that AEO from Scampton she met the last time this happened! Just like him to take advantage of another chap's misfortune.' But then he smiled to himself as he realised this couldn't happen – the Scampton crews were also tied up with this little show.

'Attention, attention, this is the Bomber Controller – for Waddington wing only, revert to readiness state one five – I repeat, for Waddington wing only, revert to one-five – Bomber Controller out.'

'Thank Heavens for that!' came a voice, accompanied by the clink of harness, as connectors were undone and harnesses were hefted back over shoulders. The relief was obvious as the aircrew reeled off their abbreviated shutdown checks and the systems wound down one at a time, ending in relative peace as the AAPP whispered to a halt and the intercom was shut down. At last silence reigned in the ears of the fed up Crew Chief as he peeled off his headphones and hung them over the nose-wheel steering jack.

With a hiss and a clunk, the entrance door dropped into the open position, and the Chief pulled down the bottom half of the ladder, reaching up to take the nav bag handed down to him from the top. The yellow painted and chipped ladder now clanked as the booted feet of the captain and co-pilot rapidly climbed down it to the ground, followed by more bags and the awkward to handle aluminium ration box and thermos flask, as the rest of the crew disembarked.

'Thanks Chief!' said the captain, a tall flight lieutenant in his late twenties, as he picked up his gear and made for the crew coach that had arrived to convey them back to the ORP huts. 'No doubt we'll be seeing you again soon'. In fact the Chief followed them onto the coach, and soon they disembarked together at the caravan that formed the servicing hub of the ORP control.

The warmth of the caravan was very welcome after the long stint out in the cold. Soon the Chief was able to peel off the outer layers of his cold-weather flying kit and check the Form 700, the aircraft servicing document, to ensure that it was still up to scratch. The aircrew, being at readiness one-five had already signed as accepting the aircraft, and this signature would stand until their shift was over.

The Chief's warming lips were now able to tell him that the latest cup of coffee was at least of drinkable temperature and he sipped it gratefully as he made light-hearted banter with the other Crew Chiefs and handlers.

There were other things that required attention, such as the H2S scanning radar system that fed the NBS (Nav Bombing System) with information that kept constant check on the position, groundspeed and track of the Vulcan. This was notorious for leakage of its nitrogen pressure. The crew entrance door-operating nitrogen-bottle pressure would also need topping up and the 3,000 PSI rapid air-starter storage bottles needed to be checked and replenished as necessary. These also leaked a little and for the expected mass rapid start of the engines on the 'scramble' command, they would need to be fully replenished. For the next twenty minutes or so, the ORP was a teeming hive of activity as various trolleys with gas bottles were towed in and out amongst the aircraft by the busy maintenance crews.

The Crew Chief ran over his checks again, plus a few more that were not in the book for good measure! In particular he checked the Ram Air Turbine stowage. The Ram Air Turbine, better known as the 'RAT', was an emergency generator that could, should main system failure occur, be extended into the airstream below the port engine air intakes of the Vulcan. It was equipped with a wind-driven turbine for generating electrical power. During the previous month, a RAT had been lost whilst airborne and a nationwide search eventually found it in a farmer's field. Thankfully this was without injury to anyone on the ground, but it was a component that he always checked now.

The Chief stretched up and ran his fingers through a trace of oily liquid that was spread over the underside of the number two engine hatches, and drew it down for a tell-tale sniff. This would identify whether or not the liquid was fuel, which would need further investigation – it was just a smear of oil. He shook the massive power and Telebrief cables which were attached to the aircraft, and checked that the steel tie-down cable fastening them to the tethered ring in the concrete apron was firmly attached. This would wrench the external power and communication lifelines free as the aircraft rolled off the ORP on the 'scramble' command. He found that all were secure. The flexible hoses to the brake units on the main bogies were checked – they had a habit of blowing oil from faulty, swaged end-fittings onto glowing brake-disc segments whilst braking. This usually resulted in a fire and that could not be tolerated, not now of all times!

He climbed the ladder into the cabin, and looked up at the three rear crew seats. The AEO position was on the starboard side, where all the electronic countermeasures and radio communications were handled. The Nav plotter sat in the centre; here was the navigational hub of the Aircraft. The Nav radar sat to port, where the bombing was set up and executed. In front of the AEO and radar positions were the wooden platforms with detachable, metal frames supporting harnesses – the so-called sixth and seventh seats, where the chief had spent many uncomfortable hours on round the world flights.

'Untidy buggers!' he thought, as he straightened out the seat harnesses of the three rear crew members, and disposed of the polystyrene drinks cups and sweetie wrappers that had been left lying about. This was obviously an oversight on the part of the bored crew, who had been on QRA for two days now – a lot of it spent at cockpit readiness of one sort or another. For instance, a readiness state of 'one-five' meant that the crew was at fifteen minutes readiness, sitting or lounging in their spartan accommodation adjacent to the ORP caravan. A readiness state of 'zero-five' meant that they were in the cockpit, door closed, with all systems running. A readiness state of 'zero-two' meant that engines were started, and with the crew's adrenaline flowing at peak they would await the Telebriefed 'scramble' order from High Wycombe that should come at any moment.

The Author in white overalls as he prepares to see off XM655 for a V.I.P. demonstration scramble at RAF Finningley.

The Crew Chief climbed up the ladder between the two Martin Baker ejection seats that provided the captain, on the port, and co-pilot, on the starboard side, with a means of emergency escape. Those crew members in the back were not so lucky, they had to exit through the door underneath, assisted by inflatable cushions on their seats, and pray that the undercarriage was not down at the time! The sixth and seventh seat passengers were even more unfortunate, as they did not have the luxury of assisted cushions, and had to rely on pure muscle power to stand and reach the door. This could be almost, if not completely, impossible under heavy 'G' forces. As the sixth and seventh seats were nominated as the first rear crew members to leave the aircraft in an emergency, they were not (officially) allowed to fly if a low-level leg was part of the flight envelope.

As the checks proceeded, harnesses were tidied, the seat and canopy safety pins checked in, and with a quick, final, look around, the Chief and his second man vacated the aircraft again for the warmth of the ORP caravan where there was more coffee waiting.

The co-pilot called in for a chat about the Chief's new car – he was thinking of buying a similar model – and the conversation developed around motor cars in general, over more coffee. The co-pilot lazily thumbed through the Form 700 checking the green line and red line entries of acceptable and deferred defects. Green line entries were for very minor defects, with which the aircraft was entirely capable of flying without immediate rectification. Red line entries were usually made by an engineering officer for more serious occurrences, and this would usually be for one flight only, such as a return to base for recti-fication. They could also be for a specified period – in the event of a routine servicing, SI (Servicing Instruction) or STI (Special Technical Instruction) having been deferred for operational necessity.

'I see that the "top hats" are still on deferred inspection,' he commented, referring to an outstanding SI pertaining to a structural NDT (Non-Destructive Testing) check that had been deferred with a red line entry. 'Top hats' referred to a part of the wing structure that looked just like a dress top hat in section, hence the rather comic name. 'Yes,' replied the Chief, 'The NDT will be carried out next time she goes into the hanger.'

The conversation turned to the coming 'Sunspot' exercise, and who was going along this time, accompanied by even more coffee.

Suddenly the klaxon adjacent to the dispersal huts blared. EeeeeeeeeeeArrh EeeeeeeeeeArrh EeeeeeeeeeeArrh – and coffee flew into the wind as the Crew Chiefs and handlers piled out of the servicing caravan door and raced for their respective aircraft. They mingled on the way with panting and cursing aircrew, running for the nearer aircraft, contorting themselves into lifejackets, struggling with their big square aluminium ration boxes and fighting to control their bulging Nav bags. The crews for the aircraft further down the ORP piled into two crew coaches to speed them on their way.

The metal door-ladders shook, clattering at contact with the metal ends of dangling hoses and attachments of their kit, as the leather-booted feet of the five crew members clambered urgently into the cabin. The AEO was always first in to fire up the necessary electrical systems, followed by the captain who initiated the sequence for eventual engine start, the co-pilot to get the fuel system in gear, the nav radar, and finally the plotter. As the last crew member entered, the ladder extension was pushed up by the Chief into its stowed position and the door was then immediately closed by the plotter, accompanied by a hiss of compressed nitrogen and a final metallic clunk as the locks slid home.

The Crew Chief pulled on his headset, which was already whining to the tune of the Telebrief as the aircraft systems came on line, and the handlers positioned themselves by each wheel, waiting to whisk the chocks away for the final launch which everyone expected was now imminent.

'Attention, attention – this is the Bomber Controller – for Wadding-ton, Scampton, and Cottesmore wings, maintain readiness state zero-five – I repeat, maintain readiness state zero-five – Bomber Controller out.'

The Telebrief whined on as everyone wondered, 'How long this time', or 'I'll bet we miss our early meal at the mess!' Early meals were always welcome, as it was there that the choicest and freshest dishes were to be served – late meals were to be avoided like the plague, as it was then that all the reheated dishes came out!

Sensing what was about to happen, the handlers kicked the wooden main wheel chocks out to forty-five degree angles against the tyres, leaving only the outboard corners in contact. This was a precautionary measure, as it was not unknown for the aircrew to run the big bomber hard up against the chocks at 'zero-two' when the engines were started, making it almost impossible to remove them without a tractor to assist – a certain demerit during a scramble. It had been known for an aircraft to roll over a chock, splintering it and lodging the remains between the wheels of the bogie. This would prevent a taxi and takeoff, whilst the damage was rectified.

The Chief looked up; the sky had become grey and overcast, and was now looking decidedly unfriendly; perhaps it would rai . . .

'Attention, attention, this is the Bomber Controller – for Waddington wing only, go to readiness zero-two – I repeat readiness zero-two – Bomber Controller out!'

Poooooowwwww – Poooooowwwww – Poooooowwwww – Poooooowwwww. The final phrase was dramatically drowned as the rapid air-starters fired almost simultaneously on all four Olympus engines. The rear view under the aircraft was lost in a shimmering haze of heat as the four mighty twin-spool turbine engines lit up, and wound, with a resonating low-pitched musical howl, through the lower rpm ranges settling out at just above idle. They were then throttled back as the aircrew ran through their final checks before the scramble that was now certain within minutes.

The handlers checked that cooling air was coming out of the outlet ducts under the engine casings – indicating this with a thumbs up to the Crew Chief. He then confirmed to the aircrew that all was well outside with a brief 'hot to trot' over the intercom. 'Thanks Chief,' came the reply.

'Attention, attention, this is the Bomber Controller – for Scampton and Cottesmore wings, come to readiness zero-two – I repeat, readiness zero-two – Bomber Controller out.'

The Chief could now imagine the explosive discharge of the rapid

A Crew Chief's eye view of a Vulcan.

air-starters and the heightened adrenaline flows at these remote loca-
tions as their V-bombers also wound up to two minutes readiness. He
could envisage very well the sense of eager anticipation in the minds
of the crews and handlers alike as they prepared themselves for a
launch into the, by now, definitely unwelcome-looking sky.

'Confirm brakes on please captain?' requested the Crew Chief.
'Confirmed,' came the affirmative reply, whereupon the Chief
signalled to the handlers to remove the chocks completely and retreat
to their safe hiding place behind the electrical plinth on the ORP.
Hopefully, this would protect them from the effects of a searing blast
of hot, acrid, choking, eye-watering jet efflux as the Vulcans at last
rolled onto the runway. 'Chocks out captain,' confirmed the Chief.

'Attention, attention, this is the Bomber Controller. For Waddington
wing only, Scramble – Capricorn. I repeat for Waddington wing only,
Scramble – Caprico . . .'

'Confirm AEO, confirm,' interrupted the captain with an urgency
fired by adrenaline, as the aircraft moved slightly toward the runway,
to be checked by the brakes with a corresponding dip of the nose. The
AEO fumbled to open the envelope containing confirmation of the
code word 'Capricorn' that would launch them.

Eventually, after what seemed an eternity, 'Confirmed, confirmed –
go, go go,' shouted the AEO in response, as the throttles opened with
the exhaust thrashing and flattening the grass for hundreds of feet
behind the concrete apron. The aircraft rolled forward; Telebrief and
power cables were separated at the same time from their sockets by
the aircraft's momentum under the restraint of the steel tie-down
cables. Throttles were eased again, as in one smooth sweep the bomber
was lined up for takeoff. With finality, the throttles were slammed fully
open, and the four Olympus 301 engines wound up to the 98.5%
power setting, thundering forth their 80,000 pounds of combined
thrust. In a cloud of oily black pungent smoke and with a mighty
roar that assaulted eardrums, even through ear protectors, the concrete
of the runway and ORP shook as the 210,000 lb. of metal and
manpower accelerated to takeoff. The front crew was thrust into their
seats, and the rear crew against their harnesses as V1, 162 knots, was
reached and the aircraft lifted off. It was closely followed by the other
three Vulcans at five-second intervals.

Ninety seconds after the command 'Scramble' was heard, the
four aircraft from the ORP were airborne and on course for their
hypothetical targets.

The Vulcans depart on a rapid scramble. The aim was for four aircraft to be airborne within three minutes from the command 'scramble'.

CHAPTER 2

A LONG HARD NIGHT: THE EXERCISE CONTINUES

The Chief never imagined that he would make early lunch after all the time consumed during the scramble, but he did, and the meal had been very welcome. The long soak in a hot bath in the Sergeants' Mess, and a much-needed change of clothes, was also welcome, but now it was time to begin the afternoon's tasks.

The Chief was sitting in a Land Rover, listening to the howl of the heavily-treaded tyres as it sped around the smooth tarmac of the perimeter track on its way back to 'Echo' dispersal. Here was the tented accommodation that was home for some of the ground servicing crews.

The runway traffic lights were on green at the 'two one' end, enabling the Land Rover to complete its journey without delay, delivering him in good time to the sprawling cluster of buildings and marquees that housed part of the station's engineering base.

There had been no news of the airborne Vulcans since the scramble and, as the weather outlook had improved, this was not really expected. With the heavy fuel loads, he could expect them to be airborne for about six hours. However, he had plenty to occupy himself with in the meantime. He was well used to 'no news' situations, as he had conditioned himself to accept the continual changes, which were an integral part of the job, without need of explanation.

He entered the Squadron Line building by the tradesmen's door and passing the control room, leant through the trade manager's counter hatch to gain a better look at the situation as portrayed on the state-boards which hung on the wall at the side of the controller's desk. He made conversation with his friend, the flight sergeant controller, whom he sometimes stood in for at certain times when he was on leave. No ETAs (estimated times of arrival) were posted, or anything else for that matter, and the topic of conversation seemed to revolve around every subject other than work. He then wandered further down the passage into the senior NCOs' crew room and made himself a mug of coffee, using the makings on the tea bar and the ever-bubbling urn of hot water.

There had been several new orders posted on the notice board, both station and squadron, so he took his coffee over and studied them as he sipped it. The 'Sunflower' exercise detail had been finally decided he noted, smiling as he saw that his name was listed amongst those Crew Chiefs chosen to participate. This was a much sought-after exercise which involved a trip to the Far East, flying the flag for Britain and participating in exercises with many foreign air forces. He thought on reading it 'Great – a nice long holiday away from this place!'

The Sunflower exercises, whilst being anything but 'holidays', were always a welcome break from routine, proceeding to the Far East in a westerly direction and known colloquially as 'westabouts' (from 'west-about reinforcement route'). They involved stopovers at places such as Goose Bay in Canada, Offut AFB in the USA, McLellan AFB at Sacramento, Hickam AFB in Honolulu, Wake Island, and Anderson (Guam). Ground servicing parties were dropped off at McLellan, Hickam, Wake and Anderson, and many a bunfight took place over who went where, as these were all very desirable places to visit. This was similar to a 'Sunspot' which was a similar trip, but only as far as the Middle East by the eastern route, and not quite so desirable. However, both Sunflowers and Sunspots were reckoned to be almost as good as 'special' rangers. Specials were trips to unusual destinations such as Thailand, Australia, New Zealand, or sometimes a Caribbean island, once again 'flying the flag' for Britain. Many an international trade or arms deal was clinched during such trips by the politicians, and the Chief and his crew were always royally entertained in the passing.

After finishing his coffee the Chief decided to wander out to 'Delta' dispersal – 'Delta 14' to be precise – and await the arrival of his Vulcan from the exercise. 'Delta' dispersal was situated on the other side of the 'Echo' dispersal buildings and formed the remainder of the eight dispersal pans that were situated in the south-easterly corner of the airfield. When the airfield was built, it was constructed on top of the old Roman Road 'Ermine Street', and the route of this old road was through the centre of 'Echo' dispersal and along the length of the main runway. The Chief often wondered what the Romans would have thought of it all if they could have seen what went on there now!

Out on the dispersal he could catch up on some outstanding paperwork, and if he had time, he could finish a couple of long outstanding letters to relatives. With a bit of luck the exercise would soon be over and he could get off the base for a well-earned night's rest at home.

It was a solitary existence in a dispersal hut, without an aircraft and its attendant ground crew to keep him company. In reality, he rather liked the lonesome existence, and when all else failed, providing the work on his aircraft was up to date and nothing else was required of him, he could get down to reading a good book during the long evenings. In the summer months he may be able to catch up on a bit of car maintenance! A Crew Chief was very much a law unto himself during the time that his aircraft was flying.

The Chief depressed the lever on the front of the Hadleigh Box to answer its squawking. 'Delta fourteen – go ahead control.'

'Your aircraft is on finals, we'll get a weapons downloading team out to you as soon as we can,' replied control.

'What else are we doing . . . how about fuel?' asked the Chief.

'Don't know yet, so we'll put it to sixty percent once your weapon is downloaded.'

Sixty percent was a good load at which to leave a Vulcan, when the required fuel load for the next sortie was not known. It didn't take a lot of work to top it up to ninety-eight percent later, which was the normal sortie load. It could be left at sixty percent, which was another common load, or de-fuelled to forty percent which was a common 'other business' load. Fuel loads were usually ninety-eight percent though, and this was always recommended instead of one hundred percent. If the tanks were filled completely and the aircraft was left standing in the sun, the fuel would expand as it heated and its specific gravity changed. It would consequently overflow. This was quite a usual happening when 'rookie' Crew Chiefs were learning the ropes, and they never forgot the merciless barracking they took afterwards – ever. One could even earn one's nickname here, which stayed with you for the rest of your time on the Vulcan force, sometimes even beyond!

The Chief looked out of his hut window and saw his handling team approaching in a Land Rover, towing a set of rapid air-replenishment bottles behind it. These would be needed during the turnaround servicing to replenish the high-pressure air-starting systems for the engines. The other equipment and nitrogen bottles were all to hand, together with the obligatory 'E to E' (Electric to Electric) generator set. This was an ingenious piece of equipment, completely mobile, and was used to generate the necessary 24 volts DC, and the 200 volts 400 cycles AC voltage that was needed to sustain the Vulcan's systems whilst on the ground. With engines shut down, it was plugged between the aircraft and an electrical plinth at the side of the dispersal. If a dispersal had an unserviceable plinth or, as sometimes was the case, no plinth at all, then Diesel ground power sets, known as 'Houchins' and having the same power outlets, were available to carry out this task.

Another glance out of the dispersal hut window took in the 'eyeballs in the sky' on the approach. This was the endearing term, borrowed from 'The Perishers' cartoon strip, and was used to describe the Vulcan's extended and illuminated landing lights, which was all that

XM655 comes in to land at RAF Finningley after the scramble and sortie is over.

could be seen from the ground as it flew the outer limits of the glide path. Control squawked to relay, 'On finals'.

The Chief checked his short lead, which would be plugged into the external intercom socket on the nose-wheel leg as soon as the Vulcan was stopped outside the dispersal. It could then be talked on into the correct position. 'Delta 14' was a rear dispersal, where the aircraft would have to be turned around after stopping by a tractor – taxi it too far on and you would not have enough room at the back of the pan to get a tractor hooked on to the towing bar! Another misdemeanour lying in wait for any inexperienced rookies.

The Vulcan touched down gracefully on the runway, like a descending bird of prey, with low pitched squeals and accompanying puffs of white smoke from the tyres. The nose was held high for a long time to make maximum use of aerodynamic braking which, with a skilful crew, could reduce the monstrous aircraft's speed to that at which it could taxi, without the tail braking parachute being deployed. This always earned the thanks of a grateful ground crew who were hard pressed enough during exercises, without having to refit this very necessary piece of equipment.

The engines whined harmonically in tune with each other, in seeming relief, as the perimeter track was negotiated, eventually turning into the 'Delta' complex of four dispersal pans. The Vulcan braked gently to a halt in the threshold of 'Delta 14', and the Crew Chief plugged in his lead as planned. The throttles were 'tweaked' by the captain, and the engines gave a brief roar to impart motion again. This faded quickly to that well-known shrill, penetrating whistle, as the bomber was 'talked' forward by the Chief, until the nose wheel was in the centre of the pan. The handlers were signalled 'chocks in', and the engines now wound down as the LP fuel cocks were closed and the crew ran through their shut-down checks.

Ground power was not plugged from the E to E set immediately, as there was already a handling team and tractor with towing bar present, having crept up behind the aircraft as it entered the dispersal. The towing bar was already being fitted to the nose-wheel leg as the aircrew vacated the aircraft.

'You'll never believe it when I tell you that we've brought the weapon back Chief,' scoffed the captain, as he and his crew piled their kit onto the newly-arrived crew coach. 'We didn't even get time to purchase any duty frees!' moaned the Nav Plotter, with a grin on his face from ear to ear.

'See you later Chief – maybe,' said the captain, as the coach started up and left the dispersal, leaving behind that unfortunate dogsbody, the co-pilot, to maintain the 'two man principle' on the aircraft which was still armed. The co-pilot was very much the 'odd job' member of the crew at times, and this no doubt is where their unfailing and somewhat laconic sense of humour was born.

The Vulcan was turned around in no time by the slick towing team, which consisted of a 'spare' Crew Chief and five men. It was correctly positioned with the nose-wheel picketing lug over the recessed steel ring set into the concrete apron. The Vulcans were always tethered with a picketing hook when at rest to prevent any untoward happenings, such as sitting them on their tail cone during refuelling! Yet another pitfall for the rookies to encounter.

After-flight checks were almost completed, and the Crew Chief reached up to turn and depress the bayonets of the fuel drain-cocks under the lower engine access panels with his screwdriver, thus draining the fuel collector boxes. This had not been a feature of earlier Vulcans and the draining fuel from engines winding down had just been left to run out onto the concrete apron. One day there was a wind blowing in the wrong direction, the fuel had blown onto overheated brakes, and the ensuing fire had destroyed the aircraft! Having said that, this procedure wasn't always the ultimate safety feature either, as the collector-drain bayonet-couplings were notorious for sticking in the open position – draining fuel just as they had done before modification.

The armament Chief in charge of the weapons off-loading team that had just arrived came into the hut and the Crew Chief gratefully signed over responsibility for the aircraft to him. This allowed the weapons off-loading procedure to commence. Bomb doors were opened and the weapon trolley positioned expertly underneath. A good team could position the trolley with an accuracy that had to be seen to be believed, and it was a matter of pride that it didn't have to be moved one iota to winch down the weapon onto it. The minihoists were hooked onto their positions in the aircraft structure and, after decommissioning, the innocuous concrete training weapon was winched down and secured to its trolley. The armament Chief then signed the aircraft back to the Crew Chief and the weapon trolley was towed away behind a Land Rover complete with its mandatory police escort. To get the weapon back to its safe storage area it had to travel across the Sleaford Road, for which the traffic was halted. It would be then moved across in front of queuing lines of vehicles, the occupants of which had absolutely no idea of what was passing by just a few yards from them.

After the procedure was completed, the co-pilot, his job done, called for transport and the fuel tanker, which had been patiently waiting, approached the starboard side of the aircraft under the watchful guidance of one of the handling crew. The driver opened the hose-reel access doors and the Crew Chief clasped the handles of the heavy pressure-refuelling hoses, one at a time, and dragged them out in a single pull. He laid them on the floor, one to each side of the aircraft. This had to be done in one pull, as the hoses were too heavy for one man to start them moving again if he stopped halfway. Also, they had to be pulled out at exactly the right amount, as connecting them onto the aircraft was difficult, and if they were too short, even by a couple of inches, fitting them was impossible. If they were too long you had the same problem, as the connector would not line up with the aircraft's refuelling coupling when the hose was bent back on itself.

The refuelling hatches, each secured by two 'dzus' fasteners (dzus fasteners were those used to secure frequently opened panels in unstressed areas, requiring simply a 90° quarter-turn to open and close), were lowered and the refuelling-coupling blanking caps were removed. The Chief, hose in both hands, climbed onto the main wheels underneath the refuelling point. The self-sealing couplings on the end of the hoses were then lifted and connected to the aircraft's refuelling nozzles with a single push and twist. This was no mean task as it meant that (for short guys) both hands were stretched high above the head with a considerable weight on them from the hose and coupling. This could be achieved easily with practice and was another job that raised howls of mirth from the bystanders when a rookie tried it for the first time. It was said that Crew Chiefs developed muscles where no one else had them!

Whilst the hoses were being coupled, the earth bonding lead was unreeled and connected by the bowser driver to the earthing point on the aircraft's structure.

The Chief then climbed the ladder, which had been positioned under the refuelling selector panel in the port undercarriage bay, and dialled up sixty percent. The system should work automatically from that point, but things could, and did go wrong here. If the automatic system didn't work correctly, the fuel could fill the rear tanks first, moving the C of G back, and sitting the bomber on its tail! This was an offence that almost guaranteed a short stay in the Tower of London at Her Majesty's expense.

It was usually better for the Crew Chief to manually operate the re-fuelling system from the cockpit, by using the electrically-operated tank valves and transfer pumps. By selecting the tanks through switches on the cockpit's mimic fuel panel, those at the front could be filled first. The percentage of fuel would be controlled by the automatic system, but the sequence of tank filling was manually controlled. The C of G meter, in the cockpit, was continually monitored to make sure that it stayed well forward. This way you stayed out of trouble.

With the fuel load at sixty percent, the hoses were disconnected, and the bowser driver reeled them in and stowed them whilst the Chief disconnected the bonding and, after replacing the blanking caps, closed the panels over the refuelling couplings by the undercarriage bays.

One last job now – read the fatigue meter! It was fortunate that this Vulcan had A and E style overload tanks fitted in the bomb bay, for these had been previously designed to fit in bomb bays when loaded with the 'Blue Steel' missile in earlier years when the Vulcan carried this type of stand-off bomb. A & E tanks had cutaways in the bottoms. This meant that when fitted to an aircraft with standard (non-Blue Steel) bomb doors, you could open the access flaps at the front of the doors and wriggle through under the A tank to the space in the centre of the bomb bay where the fatigue meter was installed. You could then read it by standing on the closed inner surface of the bomb doors. Otherwise it was read by using a pair of aluminium steps under the open bomb bay doors, and, unless you were a really tall guy or had telephoto eyes, it was extremely difficult to read that meter! Of course it could be done by pushing a hydraulic 'safety raiser' into position underneath and then pumping it up to the requisite height, but these were never to hand when you needed them.

The handlers arrived with the Form 700 from the crew debrief which had been carried out in the dispersal buildings, with two or three job cards for minor defects that had been raised by the aircrew. The tradesmen were already engaged on rectification of these and now it would only be a short while before the work was completed. Sometimes things worked so well that rectification of defects was carried out before the Form 700 arrived back from debrief; that could lead to banter with the controller over the Hadleigh box about what could be regarded as inefficiency at the debrief end.

The after-flight checks were also near completion, and the arrival of the relief Crew Chief from the oncoming shift was expected so that he could hand over his charge and get some welcome sleep. It had certainly been a long day, and his stomach had definitely decided that it was already past tea time. When he was eventually stood down he enjoyed his meal, but it was to find that he couldn't go home as

XH558 taxies in at Waddington after one of her final sorties.

XH558 shows her underside at an air show.

Vulcan XH558 gives us a view of her top surface.

XH558 – that unforgettable silhouette.

XH558 executes a fly past.

Vulcan XH558 pulls into a climb after her fly past.

Vulcan XH558 taxies at Waddington.

Vulcans lined up on their dispersal pans at Waddington on 27 March 1984.

Vulcan XH558 makes another perfect landing at Waddington on 28 April 1992.

XH558 is given an after flight servicing at Waddington on 22 November 1991.

XH558 lands at RAF Scampton on 4 October 1989.

Vulcan XH558 makes one of its final approaches.

XH558 trails its characteristic smoke as it flies sedately by.

XH558 opens its bomb doors as it turns away from the crowd at an air display, 28 May 1992.

Vulcan XH558 lined up with some sophisticated technology at Mildenhall on 28 May 1989.

XH558 trails its brake 'chute at Bruntingthorpe after its final landing on 23 March 1993.

XH558 taxies at Waddington.

Vulcan XH558 breathes a sigh of relief as it settles into its hangar for a well earned rest at Waddington.

expected, but was expected to endure another night's fitful sleep in the Sergeants' Mess.

The sound of knocking on the door of his bunk broke through a fitful sleep barrier for the Chief. 'Mmmmmmmmmh,' he moaned to himself, as he turned over and tried to ignore the invasive sounds. 'Knock, knock,' the unwelcome noise persisted. 'Yes, what is it?' mumbled the Chief, now almost fully awake.

'Chief, you are wanted at the line, both shifts have been called in. There's another flap on.'

'OK, OK,' the Chief replied, looking at his watch through bleary eyes as he snapped his bedside light on, 'I'll be right there.' It seemed but a few moments since he had closed his eyes, but his watch told him that it was 1 a.m. and he had been asleep for all of five hours.

'Not long enough,' he mused as he hurriedly pulled on his clothing and boots, tucking the laces into his boots rather than tying them. Pulling on his cold weather flying jacket, he rushed out to board the waiting Land Rover, which sped him around the airfield and deposited him once more at Echo dispersal buildings – it didn't seem like five minutes since he had left them.

Cars were drawing up from everywhere, and the Chief joined the rest of the ground crew who were hurrying into the building, ending up in a rather packed control room. The atmosphere was tense and people were being allocated jobs – disappearing out of the door for some destination or other on the airfield to complete their own small part of the jigsaw puzzle. The Chief was asked to relieve the guy on 'Echo 12' dispersal. This aircraft had returned from one of the later sorties of the exercise. Having a fair amount of fuel left, the captain had elected to carry out a few 'circuits and bumps' to use it up, as this was the most efficient way to retain currency of flying hours for the aircrew members.

He arrived on the dispersal just in time to relieve the outgoing Chief as the aircraft, XM612, was on 'finals', and the handlers arrived shortly thereafter. The planned procedure was for the aircraft to taxi into dispersal, where the co-pilot would climb out to be replaced by another aircrew member who desperately needed some currency in night flying hours; hopefully it would be a quick 'in and out' changeover.

The big bomber had just landed, and, after a perfect aerodynamic braking run, was taxiing off the runway and around the perimeter track to stop at the dispersal entrance for the Chief to plug his short lead in and talk it onto the required spot.

'Brakes,' prompted the Chief, as chocks were slid in front of the main wheels and kicked securely in, and the Chief informed the captain that all was well for the crew changeover. 'Clear door?' asked the captain. 'Clear,' responded the Chief, and the door hissed and clanked into the open position, ladder rattling as it was pulled down by one of the handlers.

The incumbent co-pilot climbed out and, whilst the replacement co-pilot enplaned, the Chief went off-line to check the flexible brake hoses on the main bogie units to make sure that there were no leaks at their swaged ends. This was a mandatory check during a 'hot' crew change with engines running, as previously several hoses had failed causing fires when the brake fluid sprayed onto the overheated brake packs. Plans were in hand to fit modified hoses, but there was a shortage of components and therefore regular checks had to be carried out. This was a dicey proposition on a 'hot' changeover such as this, as the brakes were still very hot indeed from the landing run and it was not unknown for burnt knuckles to result for any careless ground crew who were probing around in that area.

The brake hoses checked out OK, so the Chief went back on line to inform the captain that the check had been completed, by which time the new co-pilot was strapped into his seat and the aircraft was ready to roll again.

Ladder up, and the door mechanism hissed and clunked again as it shut. The chocks were kicked loose and pulled clear by the handlers. After an acknowledgement from the Chief to the captain before unplugging his external lead, the aircraft moved forward with a quick blast from the engines, rolled clockwise off the pan and around the dispersal taxiway out on to the perimeter track. The Chief sighed. One more trip, and then (hopefully) it would be time to wrap everything up for the night. He had heard that the 'flap', which necessitated the extra personnel being mustered, was now under control – this could be a nice, short, double shift after all. As the Chief wandered back to the line buildings again for his obligatory coffee his Vulcan roared off down the runway once again and away into the night sky. He sat down in the SNCOs' crew room for a read of the two-day-old newspapers that were on the table – there's nothing like old news to relieve the boredom of a double shift! He found that the extra manpower had been called in because of a short-fall in working manpower strength. This had been due to a high, but not unexpected, workload after the exercise. With the organisation quickly entering its normal 'overkill mode' there seemed (now) not to be enough work to go around to justify this. Most of that extra manpower was still sitting around waiting for jobs to be detailed. The background chatter in the crew room was suddenly disturbed by an urgent shouted message from control for the Chief to get through there – 'pronto'. He dashed down the corridor to control, accompanied by some of the others, who sensed excitement and a relief from their boredom.

'There's a Land Rover waiting outside Chief, get in it quick – 612's on fire down at "zero-one" end,' shouted the controller urgently. The Chief could hardly believe his ears as he rushed out, grabbing a long lead and headset on the way, and piled into the waiting Land Rover. In there with him he found the flight commander with a couple of handlers. They screeched out of the car park and in seconds were making a good seventy miles an hour down the perimeter track towards, what they could now see, was a fairly big conflagration. Very soon they were braking to a halt about 100 yards away from XM612, which had the underside of its port wing well alight and the fire crews just arriving. It was chaotic – as the Chief ran towards the aircraft, the crew were piling out down the ladder and running towards him, meeting him about twenty-five yards away from the bomber, which was now burning even more fiercely. The captain held out his hand, which was full of safety pins on red tags. The Chief tried to grab these as they passed each other but the majority went clattering to the floor.

'We couldn't get all the safety pins in Chief,' the captain shouted and, unbelievably, as if it were a comic strip being played out – 'Can you nip up and make them safe yourself?'

'You must be bloody well joking,' thought the Chief as he surveyed the scene, which was by now overwhelmed with firemen, who were directing light-water foam cannons on to the flames and smothering them very rapidly.

'Watch it, lads,' shouted the Crew Chief to the fire crew, 'the seats and canopy aren't safe yet, I'll get up there and do it when you let me know that it's clear.' The fire chief didn't turn around from his task, but responded with a sideways thumbs up to the Chief, who waited patiently for clearance to enter the now smouldering airframe.

After a few minutes the fire crew had finished and, with clearance, he clambered up the steps and surveyed the scene in the cabin which, hazy with a fog of acrid smoke, also contained the unmistakable odour of the foam that had been used to extinguish the flames. Through the haze the Chief couldn't see what was needed, so he climbed the ladder between the pilot's seats and gingerly leant over the live ejection seats to open the DV windows, thus letting out some of the smoke before he choked. To make it worse, the power was off, so there was no cabin lighting. He clambered out of the aircraft again to get his torch from the Land Rover, being just in time to note the arrival of Wing Commander Operations, accompanied by the station commander in his official car, complete with flying pennant – a rather incongruous sight he thought. Fortunately these officials were intent on talking to the fire crew, the junior engineering officer, and the aircraft captain who had just returned. The Chief was able to slip into his aircraft again and make the seats safe. He was amused by what he encountered there as the hastily vacating crew had done their best and fitted three of the safety pins, or so they thought; in reality they had stuffed the pins into any holes but the right ones. The Chief chuckled to himself as he made the seats and canopy properly safe and after looking out to ensure the 'brass' had left he climbed out again to survey the damage, in accompaniment with the junior engineering officer.

It was immediately obvious what had happened. Under the pressure of braking, during the first landing run since the changeover, one of the flexible hydraulic hoses to the main-wheel brake units had failed. It had sprayed hydraulic fluid from a faulty swaging onto the glowing disk packs, which had immediately ignited, quickly spreading the fire to the bogie unit. It had then rapidly spread further, from the bogie to the underside of the wing. The Doppler and Collins dielectric panels and the GRP aerial panels on the underside of the port mainplane immediately to the rear of the port undercarriage bogie then ignited, as they were immediately above the seat of the fire.

Under the extreme heat the surrounding metalwork had then started to burn and melt, and this was evidenced by a splashed trail of molten metal that stretched back along the perimeter track to the runway threshold. XM612 certainly was a sorry sight to behold. The line controller had now arrived in his car for a 'look see', no doubt to make a break from his Perspex and Chinagraph empire. It must have been soul destroying to sit in there for hours on end, knowing about everything that was happening, but never seeing it first hand. He had no doubt become very tired in there after a full twelve hours in the hot seat and felt that a trip out was just what he needed.

Immediately, the junior engineering officer made the decision to tow the aircraft to one of the dispersal pans at 'Foxtrot', adjacent to Air Traffic Control and over by the hangars where it could be inspected in detail on the following morning. As the junior engineer departed back to 'Echo' dispersal in the controller's car, the Chief supervised the water bowser that had arrived to flush away the mess of foam on the perimeter track. After this task was completed, and while he was awaiting his tug and towing team, he walked down the perimeter track to the 'zero one' threshold. As he did so, he retrieved the now cooled and hardened splashes of molten metal, chucking them inside the cabin of XM612 on his return. The Chief's expected short night was now turning into a long one indeed!

The tug seemed to take forever to arrive and now it started to rain! That's all he needed, but soon the eager team arrived and had XM612 hooked up in no time at all. They set off to 'Foxtrot' dispersal with the badly damaged aircraft where it was tethered and left for the night.

The Chief caught a Land Rover after the shift was stood down that took him to the Sergeants' mess, and his bed, at 7 a.m.! 'They'd better leave me here until at least tomorrow afternoon', he thought, as he eventually fell into a deep and well deserved sleep.

Eventually, and after much deliberation during the following week, it was decided to repair XM612 rather than to scrap it. This took a long time, as it was decided to carry out a number of modifications at the same time. These included the incorporation of some titanium 'engine containment shields'.

This was a rather expensive but necessary modification, for Olympus 300 series engines had a habit of shedding turbine discs at unfortunate moments – this had caused several fatalities and crashes. The turbine disc, usually shed at high rpm, would saw its way out of the airframe just like a massive circular saw blade causing maximum destruction, and usually fire, on its way out. If a Vulcan was airborne at the time that a disc was shed, then this was always followed by an inevitable crash. One such incident even happened during a ground engine run, where the offending disc had sawn itself out of the aircraft, and then proceeded to cut an RAF Police Land Rover into two halves. The unfortunate police dog in the back of the Land Rover was killed and the policeman in the front had a very narrow escape.

The titanium 'containment shields' were designed to be strong enough to 'contain' wayward turbine discs within the engine compartment. If they were not contained, then at least they were directed in a downward direction and out of the airframe without damaging any vital components. This was a more economical solution than modifying the engines, which were, at the time of this incident, very expensive – perhaps as much as the cost of a whole Vulcan when it was originally built.

The Chief slept all through the day and eventually arose in time for the opening of the Mess bar at 7 p.m. where he had a quick drink before going home for a meal. The following day it was work as normal, and he found himself looking after an aircraft on 'Delta' dispersal that was undergoing some rectification that had been post-poned for the exercise duration.

A sudden, and very near, massive roar of engine noise stirred him from his paperwork, and he rushed outside to see what was afoot. He pretty soon retired inside his hut again, for there was debris raining down all around him. Glass, asbestos roofing, and pieces of wood were clattering down around him and bouncing away across the dispersal – some of them rattling down on the structure of his Vulcan.

When this eventually stopped, he rushed in towards the 'Echo' dispersal building to see what was happening and saw to his amaze-ment that the row of garages that backed on to 'Echo 12' dispersal had its four walls standing, but was almost completely demolished other-wise. No roofs, no windows, and the metal roller-doors flapping in the gentle breeze.

Apparently there had been a Vulcan parked on 'Echo 12' dispersal on which engine runs had been required. Because 'Echo 12' backed on to the garages, it was not allowed to run engines at above 12% power setting for safety reasons, and this was adhered to at all times.

A Sergeant 'A Tech' had been detailed to carry out the runs and he had proceeded to do so. An 'A Tech' was a relatively new RAF trade of 'Aircraft Technician'. Entrants were normally ex-university and were trained to a high degree by the RAF; so much so that they were passed out as sergeants from their training. This created tricky situ-ations where personnel who had undergone many years of service and had climbed through the normal training and rank structure some-times felt undermined when they required an 'A Tech's' signature for the completion of their work.

Some 'A Techs' were OK and fitted in with the servicing scene as 'one of the boys', but others considered themselves a cut above the rest and behaved in a manner accordingly. The main problem was that they lacked the experience to go with their rank and some of them never seemed to improve in this respect with length of service. The 'A Tech' detailed to carry out the engine runs on 'Echo 12' was one of the latter.

He was also a rather flamboyant character, who acted in a rather ebullient manner, and at the end of each engine run that he carried out, as his signature, he always insisted on starting all four engines and 'slam checking' them. A slam check consisted of slamming the throt-tles fully open and checking how long it took for the engines to reach their full power setting afterwards. This was normally four seconds. The throttles were then returned to idling and, if all was in order, when the engines had stabilised they were shut down. This guy had only carried out a slam check on all four engines on 'Echo 12'. 'I forgot where I was,' he said afterwards. Needless to say he was severely disciplined for his indiscretion, but it never improved him.

CHAPTER 3

A CLOSE SHAVE

The day of 8 January 1971 was a day just like any other as the Chief pulled back the blinds in his bunk to let in the daylight as he prepared for another shift on the line. He was looking after a strange Vulcan this week, XM610, as its Crew Chief was on leave. His own aircraft, XM651, was in the hangar for a check servicing which meant that he was 'spare' for a few weeks. He was never too happy about the 'spare' tag, as it entailed him doing all the odd jobs that cropped up on the squadron, like being the resident Crew Chief in charge of a tugging team for turning all the aircraft that entered 'back pans' after landing. He would also get the job of supervising the teams detailed for cleaning aircraft on the wash pan, where the Vulcans were washed down about once per month to keep the finish in some sort of order. The atmospheric conditions played havoc with the high-spec paint if left uncleaned.

Today he was luckier, preparing XM610, and was in his hut awaiting the arrival of his flight crew who were rookies more or less straight from the OCU. As the weather was rather poor and their sorties on previous days had been cancelled, one of the flight commanders had joined the crew to carry out the briefing and also provide the crew with a member who had the relevant instrument rating, commensurate with the poor weather.

The crew arrived and, after their usual serviceability briefing from the Crew Chief and inspecting the aircraft, went through their normal start routine, taxied out, and were very soon airborne. After climb out, they set course for the low-level route that would form the main part of their exercise that day. Ostensibly, another routine day's work lay ahead of them, and they would be more than glad to get back later in the day, when they could debrief and look forward to an evening of leisure activities.

The first part of the low-level route went as planned, but shortly the captain reported that low cloud was obscuring the hills ahead. As the nav radar confirmed that there was ground above their flight level in that direction a decision was made to climb out to their lowest safe flight level. Engine rpm was increased from 70% to about 85% to achieve ground clearance and the nose lifted imperceptibly as a shallow climb was commenced.

As the captain completed moving the throttles forward, there was a sudden loud and heavy explosion from somewhere aft. The aircraft yawed violently and a heavy vibration set in as the port wing lifted with the aircraft going momentarily out of control.

'What the hell was that?' queried the captain loudly. 'Have we hit the ground?' This seemed the most likely answer, as they were now entering the area with higher ground and they were in and out of cloud all the time.

'No chance,' responded the co-pilot. 'We're about 1,200 to 1,800 feet above all that now.'

'Number one JPT rising,' said the captain with a touch of alarm, scanning his instruments rapidly now to gain information on what the cause might be. This was followed shortly by 'Fire in number one,' as he closed the throttle and shut off the HP cock. 'Fire drill co-pilot,' ordered the captain. 'AEO . . . get off a Mayday and prepare to abandon Aircraft.'

The rear crew, not being the first-hand recipients of the information at the fingertips of the two pilots, were beginning to suffer some small apprehensions, as events which directly involved them seemed to be unfolding in a manner that was somehow remote from them.

'Engine failure number one,' yelled the co-pilot, as he noticed the rpm on number one winding down and the fire warning light illuminating once more. 'Get number one alternator off line AEO, and give me a visual on the port wing,' ordered the captain. The AEO complied, noting that the loads on number one alternator transferred to number three without a hitch.

Looking through his periscope at the undersurfaces, he could see that number one engine was torching massively, almost like an afterburner. Three or four jets of sparks that were coming out of the joints between the engine doors joined together and formed a stream of fire almost to the trailing edge of the wing.

The fire drills were now just about complete with the co-pilot having pressed the fire extinguisher button and closed the LP fuel cock. The engine air switch was closed also, and the pumps in number one tank group switched off, as well as cross-feed cocks being checked closed. The number one JPT had risen to FSD indication and stayed there, but shortly after these checks the fire warning light went out, indicating that the fire had been extinguished.

41

'Thank heavens for that,' said the captain, but his relief was short lived. 'Number two JPT rising rapidly,' reported the co-pilot, followed by, 'Fire in number two,' and the fire drills for that engine were rapidly carried out. This was all unnoticed by the rear crew, who were by now busying themselves with ensuring that all their kit was in the correct state for an immediate bale out.

The fire drill for number two was again successful, and the fire warning light went out. The JPT was seen to be falling, but the aircraft was still difficult to fly, and the smallest tasks were even more demanding owing to the high airframe vibration levels now being experienced.

Both engine fires seemed to be under control, being confirmed by the AEO through his periscope. 'Relax guys,' said the captain, 'It looks as if we are out of the woods now,' as he sought to trim the aircraft for straight and level flight, which he found was not altogether possible.

As a precaution, the RAT was lowered by the AEO, which also shed all the non-essential electrical loads, and he then commenced to read off the FRC checklist. The captain found that he still had to wrestle with the controls, the big bomber now bucking and yawing its way through the sky. The captain had full throttle applied to numbers three and four engines which climbed the aircraft slowly, as he wanted to gain as much height as possible to give his rear crew a better chance in the event of them having to bale out. This possibility was becoming less likely as he found that he was gaining some form of control over his aircraft and would possibly be able to attempt a landing somewhere.

The AEO now checked his periscope again and was horrified to see that there was a fire started again underneath the port wing, which was now completely covered in flames. 'Captain . . . we're torching like hell now under one and two engines . . . what are your indications?'

'None up here,' responded the captain, which seemed to indicate that the electrics to the warning circuits were now burned through, but that seemed irrelevant in the light of the current revelation from the AEO.

The AAPP was now started by the AEO just in case its electrical output should be needed, and he put out another Mayday call to Scottish AATC as the captain selected emergency IFF and informed the crew that the order to abandon aircraft was imminent.

It was now becoming increasingly difficult to hold the aircraft, but the captain found that he could still trim it to fly straight and level, albeit with a very high level of vibration at 240 knots, and this bode well for the rear crew baling out. Being at 9,000 feet altitude also meant that they would not require oxygen, and so the hoses were disconnected preparatory to leaving the aircraft. More and more power was now required to maintain the status quo, and this was only achieved by using 95% power on the two remaining engines. The captain informed the rear crew that he would order them to abandon aircraft when he could see a break in the cloud cover below. This would ensure that they were in an area that would be reasonably safe and a full check of their safety equipment was now made yet again.

The abandonment decision was formalised by the illumination of the 'abandon aircraft' panel lights on the rear console. The nav radar, being nominated the first to go, looked at the other two with a resigned expression on his face and, projected by his assisted cushion, vaulted on to the door. It was difficult to get hold of the handle to open the door owing to the now very high level of vibration being experienced, but eventually he managed it, slamming it through the emergency gate. There was a sudden roar, as the door cracked open and a gap of six inches appeared but no more, and slowly the door closed again until a gap of only about an inch was to be seen. The nav radar looked at it in disbelief, looking in dismay at the nav plotter who was the one with the other means of opening the door. As it was no use shouting, for the noise level in the cabin was now too high, the nav radar gesticulated wildly to the door at the same time as the nav plotter realised what was wrong and operated his switch also. The door now moved rapidly to the fully open position, but escape was still barred by something which was stretched across the door opening from jack to jack, probably the door seal which had become detached. Try as he might the nav radar could not dislodge this, but suddenly it was gone – whipped away in the howling slipstream that was roaring past the open door. The glow of the fire could now be seen reflected in the metalwork of the door. The nav radar felt an overwhelming urge to leave the aircraft now before anything else went wrong and, taking a deep breath, he launched himself down the door and into the turbulent air and safety. The AEO was next and he certainly didn't waste any time, operating his seat air-bottle to lift him by means of his assisted cushion, followed shortly by the nav plotter, who was probably least worried of all the crew, being a sport parachutist! This was his thirtieth jump.

With the rear crew gone, the captain concentrated on flying his aircraft. He knew that he was in the vicinity of Hartlepool and if at all possible he would like to get his aircraft nearer the coast and heading out to sea before abandoning, but at this time consideration was once more being given to a safe landing, possibly at Leeming.

Hydraulic pressure was now at zero, so it was obvious that the oil had all been lost through severed pipes, possibly even feeding the fire. The captain now attempted some low-speed handling checks but soon abandoned these when a heavy buffet developed and the aircraft shook violently, almost going out of control.

The captain found that it was becoming increasingly difficult to hold the control column now, as aching muscles complained, and it was becoming obvious that a safe landing was out of the question. A safe landing had really been out of the question all along, but in times like this the mind will think along all avenues to salvage the situation, when the real solution is to get out as quickly as possible!

Both pilots now reached for their bonedomes, which had been forgotten in the execution of their unexpected workloads, and these were fastened to the grab handles at the rear of the ejection seats. The captain indicated to the co-pilot that he was about to jettison the canopy which then separated cleanly from the aircraft. The noise level now increased somewhat, but both pilots were surprised that no buffet or high wind levels were experienced in the open cockpit. Having a more open view with the canopy gone, and looking around, the Captain was horrified at the sight that greeted him. The conflagration over the wing upper surface was far worse than that which had been seen on the underside. Whilst the area forward of the main spar appeared quite normal, the rest of the upper surface of the wing now seemed to be one mass of flames, being fanned to blast furnace intensity by the 220 knot airflow over the aircraft. The dense smoke trail was being whipped up over the roof of the bomb bay by the sideslip that was now being experienced and the fin could be seen sticking incongruously out from the top of the smoke.

It was obvious that both remaining crew members must get out as soon as possible, as the airframe was now being violently rocked, accompanied by rumbles, as the port fuel tanks began to explode. With considerable difficulty the aircraft was trimmed straight and level and headed out to sea. The captain indicated to the co-pilot for him to get out. The co-pilot reached up to pull his face-blind handle and realised that at that high level on the seat there was considerable air turbulence. As he pulled the blind, his right hand was deflected from the handle, which came out at an angle, and the seat did not fire. Panic gripped him momentarily as he frantically scrabbled for the handle again, which this time pulled out fully and he felt a reassuring thump accompanied with a smell of cordite as the seat cartridges fired and lifted him clear of the doomed Vulcan.

The captain checked once more that all was well with the attitude and direction of the aircraft and grasped his own face-blind handle, pulling it successfully and making a timely explosive exit. Descending on his parachute, he twisted around, becoming aware that his back had suffered a compression injury during ejection, to see what had become of his Vulcan. He saw to his dismay that it was now in a vertical dive and shedding large pieces of structure and dense black smoke as it plunged toward the ground. He followed it down visually until impact, which hopefully had missed some houses that he could see were in the vicinity, and with a large mushroom of black smoke, everything was obscured from his view – this was very definitely the end for XM610.

Back at base, the Chief was called into the flight commander's office and informed of the tragedy, which shocked him very much, but he was pleased to hear that no lives had been lost, for that was always the danger in incidents like this. It reminded the Chief that what they all did for their living was not a mundane job, as they sometimes looked at it, but a highly dangerous job where personnel had been killed and would continue to be in the future.

He was asked to get his kit together for a few days and accompany the AIB team to the crash site to help in the investigation. It was already strongly suspected that a turbine disc failure had contributed to the demise of XM610 and evidence was being sought to confirm this. XM610's engines had not been modified in respect of turbine disc

The hole was dug by XM610 at Wingate when it crashed. The leader of the accident investigation team referred to it as 'a typical Vulcan hole'.

failure prevention, nor had it containment shields fitted. These were modifications that would take a long time to wholly incorporate into the Vulcan fleet, but thankfully, disastrous events, such had overcome XM610, were very rare.

The Chief took his own car up to Hartlepool, in company with a sergeant electrician who had quickly volunteered as he was a native Geordie. They checked in at the Grand Hotel with the rest of the AIB team, departing immediately thereafter for the crash site.

The Vulcan had crashed on a slight incline in a piece of waste ground that was literally surrounded by houses and the Chief marvelled that luck could not have dealt their inhabitants a better hand. Had the Vulcan piled-in a hundred yards in any direction, the death toll of civilians could have been quite high.

It was a dismal day, with rain falling steadily as the Chief surveyed the scene. There were caterpillar-tracked vehicles of the REME in evidence, which had been called in to attempt to recover the engines which were suspected to be buried up to fifty feet down in the soft ground. These vehicles had transformed the locality into a virtual mire. The 'Vulcan hole' (as the leader of the AIB team called it), was about 150 feet long by about 40 feet wide, and 20 feet deep. It was full of debris and what appeared to be water, but as the Chief neared, the smell told him it was something else! The main sewer had been fractured, and raw sewage was flooding the hole – what a job this was going to be!

Looking around the site, the Chief noted the rather comical sight of the ECM (electronics countermeasures) cans, which are carried in the tail of the Vulcan. These had been thrown out as the fuselage disintegrated, and were all 'planted' up the slope in a straight line. Other than these, the only recognisable bit was a piece of wing skin about five feet square that was lying in amongst the millions of smaller pieces of debris that littered the area. Apart from this single recognisable piece, all the other fragments measured but a few square inches apiece.

The main concern was to locate the NBS film cassette which was a piece of highly classified equipment. This contained the bombing characteristics of the sortie. It was normally housed in the NBS equipment and fed information to the rudimentary computer that calculated the bombing parameters, and to this end an intensive search was initiated. They could not believe their luck when after two days the film was found and taken back to Waddington.

After a few more days of futile tramping around the wreck site the Chief returned to Waddington, where the board of enquiry would establish its findings. The stay at the Grand Hotel was not as 'grand' as it may have at first seemed. They had an early breakfast each morning and were off to the crash site at 7 a.m. and did not return until about 8 p.m. when it was straight in to a late dinner, which was laid on in a segregated part of the dining room. This was done because of the state of the crash site and their general wet and muddy condition! When the Chief checked out of the Grand he also found it a little strange, as although he had been paid his 'rate ones' for accommodation, he was just asked to sign his bill, and on querying this was simply told that it was what the others were doing! (The 'others' being all RAF and Army officers, and civilians from the AIB.)

At the final sitting of the board of inquiry, this was mentioned in passing. The wing commander and the squadron leader looked at each other as the light dawned, and the squadron leader muttered, 'So that's why our bills were so high!'

The Chief had to laugh about it afterwards really, as it meant that the officers had unwittingly paid his hotel bill for him, whilst he had pocketed his 'rate ones'!

The final result of the board of enquiry confirmed the suspicions of the initial inquiry; that number two engine had shed a turbine blade, which had subsequently wrecked the whole of the disc, eventually causing the shedding of the complete LP turbine disc. The debris had penetrated and caused a similar failure in number two engine, and with the fuel tanks ruptured and on fire, the inevitable crash was a foregone conclusion.

One 'small' thing that came to light was that the navigator's parachute harness came unfastened when he stood up after landing. This was caused by incorrect maintenance procedures, but showed just how lucky he was to get away with his aircraft abandonment and live.

Sometimes lightning does strike the same ground twice however, as some time later, in Malta, the same Vulcan captain had another unfortunate experience with a Vulcan that was lost, complete with three rear crew and two crew chiefs as a result. Every time something like that happened the Chief was brought to think about his own mortality for a while, but eventually all fears were pushed into the background, as this was a very rewarding job and one he would swap for no other.

CHAPTER 4

THE *TIRPITZ* INCIDENT

Occasionally, the Waddington scene was broken by incidents that involved visiting aircraft and late January 1971 was no exception when a IX Squadron Vulcan was prepared for a 'UK ranger' by NEAF Bomber Wing.

'It will be nice to get a break in the UK,' thought the captain, as his Akrotiri-based Vulcan began its descent into Waddington. The sighing aerodynamic noise from the aircraft changed significantly and buffet was felt, as the undercarriage extended into the air-stream and air-brakes were selected to high drag to slow the Vulcan on its approach. During the finals 140 knots was maintained, reducing to 130 knots over the threshold with the main wheels contacting the runway shortly thereafter, accompanied by puffs of smoke and squeals of tortured rubber as they wound up to speed. The nose was held high to make maximum use of aerodynamic braking, for they didn't want to stream the brake 'chute on this one, as it would only mean an inconvenient repackaging job for the two Crew Chiefs who accompanied them. Not only that, if it was damaged it would have to be replaced and, knowing what they had planned, this would be doubly inconvenient if Waddington would not oblige – Cyprus would have to send one over. Eighty-five knots and the nose-wheel was lowered gently to the runway, and very soon they were making a gentle right sweep onto the perimeter track that would take them around to the visiting aircraft dispersal at 'Foxtrot'.

The crew disembarked with their kit after shutdown checks were completed for the ops block, leaving the Vulcan in the capable hands of the two Crew Chiefs that had accompanied them on this trip. The Crew Chiefs' plans were to ready the aircraft and then get off to their respective UK homes for couple of days' break in an English winter. With their normal existence of Cyprus sunshine they must have been mad.

They were on a specific mission from Akrotiri in Cyprus, with set tasks to carry out, but above all, this trip had a much darker agenda –

an operation that would go down in the annals of RAF history as legendary. Their real mission was to raid 617 (Dambuster) Squadron at Scampton to retrieve the trophy of the Tirpitz bulkhead that had been stolen from them earlier under shady circumstances on 7 January 1971, when a truce had allegedly been declared for a VIP visit. The station commander at Akrotiri had stated that it was to be retrieved whatever the cost.

During WW2, both 617 and IX Squadrons had been credited with the sinking of the German battleship *Tirpitz,* which had been sheltering in a Norwegian fjord. After the war, the Norwegian Government had presented a bulkhead from the battleship to both IX and 617 Squadrons to share between them. One trophy between two Squadrons was almost the catalyst for WW3 and the competition between the Squadrons as to who had possession of this trophy was intense. Not only the station commander at Akrotiri, but IX Squadron themselves were smarting from 617's success, and were determined to get it back. Therefore, before their departure on the UK ranger, the OC IX Squadron had asked the captain to employ all means at his disposal to retrieve the bulkhead whilst they were in the UK, and this

The IX Squadron badge.

The IX Squadron badge.

he was determined to do. Most of the crew were blissfully unaware of what the captain and his co-pilot were plotting and most departed, along with the Crew Chiefs, for destinations of their own to visit relatives and friends elsewhere in the UK. This left the captain and his co-pilot to carry out the recovery between them.

Obviously, the first task for the pair was to locate the bulkhead at Scampton without arousing any undue interest that might highlight their presence. In this, they had a ready-made excuse to visit the station, as the captain was shortly to join the OCU (Operational Conversion Unit) there as an instructor. He would visit, introduce himself to his colleagues-to-be, check the lie of the land and seek out some ex-IX Squadron compatriots that he knew were presently at Scampton, who might help him.

A Transit van was hired from SHS (a well known hire firm in those days) in Lincoln and they proceeded to Scampton in this and pretty soon made themselves at home in the offices of 230 OCU. Over coffee, they manoeuvred conversation around (nobody knew they were from IX Squadron apparently) to how well 617 had done in stealing the bulkhead and eventually asked if they could see it. They were told by the squadron leader that it was not on view at the moment, as it was actually in station workshops, in the carpenters shop, being refurbished. When it was found that they had a transit van with them, the light began to dawn on 230 OCU what the real purpose of their visit was.

It didn't take them long to locate the bulkhead but, whilst attempting to gain entry to the locked building, they were almost caught in the act by a very vigilant senior aircraftman, who tried to persuade them not to remove it until his sergeant came back. They had told him a cock and bull story that it was required for a party at the officers' mess!

Irrespective of further protests from the airman, the bulkhead was loaded, and they set off for Waddington, assuming that they had a couple of hours start (at least) to get it secreted into the 4,000 lb. pannier that was in the Vulcan's bomb bay. They soon realised that this would not be possible when, after a refuelling stop at a garage, they found that 617 Squadron was in hot pursuit. A desperate chase around the Lincolnshire roads resulted where they eventually managed to evade the pursuing vehicle and its irate incumbents.

They now realised that their IX Squadron Vulcan at Waddington would have 617 guys swarming all over it; it would be impossible to load the bulkhead and another plan would have to be devised. Such a plan was quickly formulated and this involved depositing the bulkhead at another airfield for storage. After takeoff from Waddington, they could then make an unauthorised diversion, pick it up, and be away to Cyprus with their trophy.

Cranwell was briefly considered, and then Cottesmore, but the captain didn't know anyone there. If 617 Squadron got wind of it, they would go there, remove the bulkhead, and when he arrived to pick it up it would be gone. It wasn't worth all the flak and repercussions that this might cause without having the bulkhead to show for it when he got back to Cyprus.

The captain had a brainwave, and decided to enlist the help of a WRAF officer friend, whom he had met out in Cyprus (and whom he appeared to fancy more than a little) – he felt that she would help him. She was presently at Spitalgate, so they drove over there and made contact at her office. The captain explained the situation to her, pouring out all of his plans. He asked her to drive another vehicle, that he would hire, and into this they would transfer the bulkhead. All she would have to do would be to drive the vehicle to Cottesmore the next day, and meet them at an appointed time when they would have landed their Vulcan. The bulkhead could then be swapped into the pannier. He also thought that, when he came back to UK in a few months time to take up his new post at Scampton, it would be a good excuse to thank her by taking her out to dinner and hope for further developments. He was devastated when she turned him down flat – and threatened to tell 617 Squadron of his plans into the bargain!

With all his plans in disarray, the captain returned to his co-pilot and the rented van to decide what to do. He couldn't use Cottesmore now under any circumstances, as the uncooperative WRAF 'friend' knew all about it. If 617 got wind that he was to use another station to divert to and pick up his booty, they had enough personnel to send a party to all of the possible airfields to prevent him loading it. They could also blow the gaff on his unauthorised diversion plans and then he would be in big trouble!

Eventually, after weighing up all the possibilities, he decided on Wittering, and the bulkhead was taken there in the van and deposited in the Receipt and Dispatch department with a label saying that it would be picked up by so and so on the next day.

Obviously a lot of thinking had been done by the pair during their drive about the Lincolnshire countryside and they were hoping against hope that nothing vital to the success of their plans had been left out. The new plan was to land at Wittering as soon as possible after takeoff from Waddington, having burnt off enough fuel to be at a reasonable landing weight, and take a chance that 617 wouldn't saturate all stations with personnel as he feared. This could be a tricky landing and, what was more, he didn't want to stream the brake 'chute, as that would unnecessarily delay him.

One immediate problem was that Wittering, being a Harrier base, was landing with prior permission only, but that was a 'minor' problem that he felt could easily be overcome. Another problem was that, after burning off fuel, he would need a re-fuel to get back to Cyprus. What if Wittering wouldn't, or couldn't, oblige? If they couldn't re-fuel him, the next plan for this stage was that he would have to get airborne from Wittering and land at either Wildenrath in Germany, or Malta in the Med for his fuel top up.

Deciding to complete some checks with Wittering Tower to assess the feasibility of his plans, the captain ascertained that Wittering would accept a PD (Practice Diversion), but that the circuit density (traffic) might be high, especially on the planned day. This could make things tricky, and so he decided to put off his trip until the next day when things would not be so busy. This he could easily do, as he had arranged an operational recall to be sent to him from Akrotiri – this meant that he could choose his own departure time. Meantime, he could keep 617 busy thinking that it was at Waddington that he was to load the bulkhead. At this point, only the captain and his co-pilot knew the real plan. The rest of the crew knew something was afoot, but not how complicated it had all become. There were some misgivings, as by now the Crew Chiefs had got wind of intrigue, and one of them approached the captain and asked outright what was going on. He told the captain that a wing commander (most probably the wing commander of 617 Squadron) had offered him a barrel of beer if he would tell him where the bulkhead was! He hadn't a clue what the chap was talking about. He was told not to worry as everything was under control.

They returned to Waddington and getting back to their rooms in the Mess to pick up their kit, the captain and co-pilot found that it had been given a good search by 617. Items of flying clothing and some flying manuals had been taken, obviously in an effort to stop them leaving on time. Even the service police didn't want to interfere, as by now Waddington had got wind that something was up, as OC 617 was there with a number of his crews, and the beans had been well and truly spilt so to speak. However, the important thing was to keep 617 guessing, in the belief that the bulkhead was somewhere at Waddington, and that the captain was still going to make an attempt to load it before that evening's planned takeoff.

The subterfuge continued throughout the early evening, and the Wing Commander Operations was getting a little tetchy about what was happening around him. He obviously didn't like the interference from Scampton, but he tended to side with them rather than with the IX Squadron captain. After all, Scampton was their neighbouring station, and Cyprus was a million miles away! It was also probably because he wished that all this upset to his usual routine would quietly go away, but felt that a solution was out of his personal reach. Several acid exchanges took place between the Wing Commander Ops and the captain, who went out to his aircraft to see how preparations for takeoff were going. The pannier was not hoisted and space had been made for a large box of saddles that they had agreed to take back for the riding school in Cyprus. This would have 617 guessing when it arrived! They now fully expected that preparations were being made to load the bulkhead.

There were now about forty aircrew members of 617 Squadron milling around his aircraft, all of them expecting the bulkhead to arrive at any time, and when the box of saddles arrived they thought that they had hit the jackpot. Men from 617 tried to break it open, whilst the Crew Chiefs tried to protect it, and the service police in attendance didn't appear to know what to do about it. Bribes of money were offered from both sides, but there were no takers. Eventually things calmed down, the pannier was still on the ground (without the bulkhead) and 617 began to feel in a more buoyant mood. With the captain's impending departure time getting nearer, they felt that no way could the IX Squadron crew load the bulkhead now with them present – they had won.

The captain's own crew was becoming decidedly uneasy now, as they felt that takeoff time was approaching, and no real moves were being made to finish the final planning etc. They also strongly suspected that their captain and co-pilot had the bulkhead, so how were they planning to load it, when were they planning to load it, and most importantly how?

The time continued to pass, and there was yet another acid exchange between the captain and the Wing Commander Operations about the impending departure time (that had not been confirmed), and he literally thumped the table and asked, 'Are you bloody well going or not?' The captain, still stalling, said that he couldn't possibly go until his kit and flying manuals had been returned, and that he would soon have to signal Cyprus to say that he was being delayed because of 'administrative reasons'. Everyone knew that would provoke stern inquiries from Cyprus which would be hard to explain.

Eventually, all the stolen kit was returned after a phone call from the

Wing Commander Operations (presumably to the 617 guys), and the captain then took the opportunity that all the messing about had provided to delay his takeoff until 10.00 the next morning. The official reason – crew fatigue. The plotter had travelled all the way from Cornwall and was feeling tired.

Not being party to the captain's plan, the plotter and the rest of the crew were very unhappy about this, but nevertheless had to comply. The 617 members were told of the changed takeoff arrangements, but they only half believed it, thinking that it was a ploy to try and get rid of them so that the captain could load his spoils and get airborne that night anyway. Against this view was that an exercise was planned for the next day that would keep 617 busy and stop them from fully guarding his aircraft. This could be seen as the captain's real opportunity to load the bulkhead and get clean away. Ultimately, the captain and his crew retired to their messes, feeling that they had done a very good job in deceiving 617 as to their true intentions, and given them a good messing about into the bargain.

The next day they arose and, after breakfast, proceeded with a check of the aircraft, and then went into the self-briefing room to make their flight plans. Discreet checks were made with Wittering to ensure that the correct ground power units and fuel were available, and it was then that the first fly in the ointment was discovered. It was confirmed that they wouldn't be allowed to land at Wittering without prior permission – the captain made up his mind that he would go there anyway, on his practice diversion, and force his way in regardless!

Irrespective of the exercise, 617 were still guarding his aircraft, but in very much reduced numbers – one to be precise, and he had installed himself in an 'Ice Box' (a small hut on wheels that the ground crew normally use in hangars as an administrative facility). Because there were things afoot that his crew did not know, and should be told by now, the captain relented and told the plotter that he would be declaring a change in flight plan to them all after takeoff. He would be flying north to burn off fuel and wanted to be back overhead at Waddington one hour after takeoff. He had calculated that by then he would be down to an acceptable landing weight for Wittering and could safely land without his tail breaking 'chute having to be deployed. His crew now began to sense victory in the air.

The final checks of the aircraft revealed that 617 Squadron had been at work in the early hours, for fuses were missing from vital pieces of equipment and it wouldn't start. More delaying tactics on their behalf that wouldn't do them one bit of good! The Chiefs were asked to replace the fuses and to do a full check to make sure that nothing else vital was amiss.

The captain suddenly noticed that the winches for the pannier were all marked in a Waddington coding – as he would need to lower his pannier at Wittering, where were his own winches? The Crew Chief looked surprised and said that they hadn't been brought along, as they always borrowed Waddington's. This was a blow indeed, and he told the Crew Chief that when they left it would be with Waddington's winches on board. The Chief smiled, with a light of understanding dawning on his face as he realised what was afoot – no further questions were asked.

Another check was made, that of ensuring that enough rapid air was carried, and here he was dealt another blow, as Waddington had used all of theirs for the exercise and there was none available to charge the IX Squadron Vulcan's systems. There was enough in the tanks for one rapid start after leaving Waddington – this was going to complicate matters! If Wittering couldn't refuel him, he would need to keep this rapid air for a start at either Wildenrath or Luqa. This meant that he would have to keep an engine running all the time whilst he was on the ground at Wittering – rather difficult to do when he thought of the circumstances under which he was going to force his way in there!

Eventually, everything was sorted out to the captain's liking, and there was even a humorous incident when the 617 resident spy was secured into his 'ice box'. This was done at the side of the dispersal by binding lashing tape around it and tying engine intake blanks over the windows so that he could not see out. For his benefit a stage play in sound was then enacted by the IX Squadron crew to simulate the loading of the bulkhead! Pure and utter pantomime for 617's benefit.

The time came for crew checks and engine start, and bidding farewell to the 617 spy. He was now free and accompanied by a service policeman who had made an attempt to search the IX Squadron Vulcan without success. They taxied out and were airborne in next to no time at all, bound (as far as Waddington was concerned) for Akrotiri.

After ATC handover, they turned north, descended to 20,000 feet, lowered the undercarriage, selected high-drag airbrakes, and commenced to burn off fuel at a high rate. Finally, the crew was let in on the secret, but not as to how the captain planned to force his way in to Wittering – he didn't want a riot on his hands just yet.

An hour later, fuel looking at a reasonable level for landing, they were heading for Wittering, who were called up and asked for a practice diversion, with a PAR, and a roller landing. Wittering informed the captain that they couldn't accept a roller, as their crash establishment was not up to the required level, and this was acknowledged and an overshoot was accepted. At 1,000 feet, the captain declared his (fabricated) minor emergency, requesting an immediate landing.

Actually, in truth the aircraft didn't feel right at that point. It was yawing and felt very sloppy in control response. They were, the captain now realised, also very heavy (miscalculation over fuel), too fast, and would have to give the brakes a caning on landing – but the decisions, which were irreversible, had now been made.

The touchdown was made on the runway threshold and it was soon obvious that there was still too much speed on, and the runway markers flashed by at a speed that necessitated really heavy braking. They soon had the tower reporting heavy smoke from the bogies. The end of the runway was reached and they were still too fast, necessitating a very rapid left turn off and onto the perimeter track, being now hotly pursued by fire tenders and ambulances.

They now found themselves being directed into a dispersal, to find that there were no suitable chocks available and this created a further problem for them. With overheated brakes, they dare not put the brakes on and leave them on, as the discs and pads would weld together. They also couldn't shut engines down, otherwise the fuel that might dribble from the collector box drains would fall onto the bogies and a fire would result. The collector boxes had been modified to prevent this happening with the addition of bayonet-operated drains, but these always stuck and may as well not have been fitted. The captain was obliged therefore to keep moving slowly, applying his brakes on and off, with one of the Crew Chiefs outside monitoring progress. The external intercom decided to fail at this moment and the nav radar got out to see what was happening. He found that the port bogie was very hot and covered in extinguisher powder, and he reported back that under no account were engines to be shut down yet. All this created some consternation at Wittering station level, and by now the station commander's car was in evidence with pennant flying at the scene. The tower was asking why they couldn't shut down engines, and the situation was becoming very fraught and very public – the last thing that was wanted.

Eventually chocks were found, engines shut down, and suitable explanations found for the powers-that-be, who were in fact falling over themselves to be helpful. 'Where had they come from?' An awkward question that could scupper their plans. 'Akrotiri,' came their reply, whereupon surprise was expressed in the tower until they explained they were in fact an Akrotiri aircraft en route from

Waddington to Akrotiri. The tower wanted to know if all parties should be informed, especially as they had declared to Wittering that their planned refuelling stop was to have been Wattisham. The captain said that was not necessary, as they had already informed all parties concerned by radio. They quoted SSB radio to the tower, as this was the latest 'in' kit at the time (that the Vulcan was not fitted with), and held in some awe by all who encountered it. However, this was accepted without question and they all breathed a sigh of relief.

Things were now looking good, nobody outside of Wittering knew where they were, the brakes had cooled, they could shut down, and they had been promised fuel. All they had to do was to convince the powers-that-be that the 'problem' that had caused their emergency landing could be fixed by the Crew Chiefs, and they were home and dry.

The captain climbed out and introduced himself to the station commander, stating that their emergency had been occasioned by a bomb bay overheat. This was caused by a sticky hot-air valve and the resultant escape of hot air could affect the flying controls. It was a common fault that the Crew Chiefs could quickly fix without any assistance and, after refuelling, they could soon be on their way. The repairs would mean that the pannier had to be lowered, but they required no assistance for this either. All that was needed was the loan of a vehicle to drive the plotter about to file his flight plans. They needed nothing further. Things were looking even better!

The vehicle arrived and, after filing his flight plans, the captain and the plotter realised that a bigger vehicle than the present Land Rover was required to collect the bulkhead, so a larger one was requested and obtained. They went to stores and picked up the bulkhead, taking it out to the aircraft, where the Chiefs had the pannier lowered and waiting. It was quickly loaded and the pannier winched back up into the bomb bay. Even the NAAFI wagon arrived with refreshments and they all began to relax a little as their plans had so very nearly come to fruition. A wary eye was kept out – just in case 617 had got wind of where they were and tried to make a last ditch attempt to stop them getting away.

A power set arrived and was connected, and shortly afterwards the fuel arrived. They couldn't persuade the power set to work however, so refuelling was carried out using the AAPP, and (would you believe it?) the Padre turned up for a chat about times gone by when elements of the V-Force were based at Wittering.

The Form 700 was completed with the results of the inspection on their faulty hot-air valve (that was now miraculously found to be serviceable), refuelling completed and preparations made to start up and get airborne with their precious cargo. Fuel delivery had been a little short and this meant that the C of G was a little forward, but this was quickly rectified by using the internal pumps to move fuel about, and very soon they were airborne and en route for Akrotiri. Mission accomplished.

They all felt that, when the UK stations realised what had been going on, there would be repercussions, and this was the case. A letter was received by the Wing Commander Bomber Ops at Akrotiri, from the Wing Commander Operations at Wittering, stating in no uncertain terms that he did not appreciate what had happened, but, under the circumstances, he was leaving it to the authorities at Akrotiri to deal with. A very understanding man, the captain and his crew all felt, as it was under the instigation of these very 'Akrotiri authorities' that the whole plan had been devised and executed.

CHAPTER 5

SWING SHIFT

Time had rolled by, it was mid-1972 now and thankfully the concept of centralised servicing had at last been consigned to the dustbin. Hard lessons had been learned and morale had hit hidden depths but now the Chief, along with many of his colleagues, was assigned to a squadron. His new outfit was number 101 Squadron, and not only did it have its own ground crew, but its aircraft were emblazoned with the squadron badge and all was going very well indeed.

For June, it was a cold and rainy night on the airfield and the Chief was on swing shift, which made him feel a whole lot better about it! A mist was forming due to cold rain meeting the warmer ground and this was starting to rise around the Vulcan bombers. They sat shiny and dripping in the yellow enveloping glow of the sodium security lights, reflected in the water on the pan surface as it puddled below their mighty airframes.

It reminded the Crew Chief of his first ever sight of the Vulcans at Waddington Airfield, on a night not too dissimilar to this, during November 1969, as he approached across the surrounding country-side to join the station for the first time. The Vulcans were then to be seen parked on their distant dispersals, illuminated by the ghostly glow of these very sodium lamps, somehow branding them as menacing and secretive in their lairs.

He was a brand new 'rookie' Crew Chief then, about to complete the final phase of his training at Waddington, being straight from the last of his series of training courses, all of which had taken up the best part of a year of his service.

The job of a V-Force Crew Chief was legendary throughout the Air Force and many stories were recounted about Chiefs in the early years being so overloaded with work and responsibility that nervous break-downs and other stress-related invalidities were reputed to be the norm.

He held the rank of sergeant and was stationed at Benson in Oxfordshire when he found out that he was selected for ASC training.

Being established on first-line servicing with Argosy transport aircraft, he had great misgivings at first – especially when colleagues shook their heads in sympathy when they heard about it. However, he decided to go along with it as the job carried accelerated promotion to Chief Technician, and a substantial pay rise to boot. In later years he was glad that he stayed with it, as now that the relentless pressure associated with a primary strike force had been somewhat relieved, so had the massive workload that went with it. In the end, it did turn out to be the most satisfying and rewarding job that he had ever done.

Being an Aircraft Fitter (Airframe) by trade, the course had started for him at St Athan, in South Wales. Here he learnt about the Olympus engine propulsion system; following on to Newton in Nottingham-shire, where he was taught electronics and instrumentation; finishing at Finningley, where all the teaching and theory of the previous months was put together into practice on the Vulcan bomber itself.

Mentally, it had been a very hard course and now he was looking forward to getting to grips with the job, which he knew would be very challenging and, he hoped, rewarding. He had made many friends during his time at the Vulcan training schools, tragically to lose some of them to fatal accidents some time later.

It was three years later now and in many respects the job had surpassed all expectations. As already mentioned, he was working the boring 'swing shift' this week. This was the stint from twelve midnight until 8 a.m. the following morning, when the day shift would come in to relieve him.

This shift was a killer, as your system never really got used to working a week of days followed by a week of nights, and every fourth week a 'swing shift'. This shift was alright as conceived, for it was purely to prepare aircraft for the next day's sorties, but the concept was very much abused now. Due to the current defence cuts the day shifts were very much undermanned and the never-ending slog of rectification tasks were now being finished off by the 'swing shift'. This kept them very busy indeed as it was on top of their allotted primary tasks of aircraft preparation.

The Chief had several aircraft to oversee that night, which were being prepared for the following day's flying programme. Fuel loads were being adjusted, bombs loaded, and before-flight inspections being carried out. This kept him very busy indeed, as the next day was going to be a maximum effort, live bombing exercise over the North Sea Range. For this the Chief's own aircraft, XM651, plus the others selected had been placed into the conventional bombing role and loaded up with twenty-one 1,000 lb. 'iron' bombs. XM651 was now

The Chief's very own Vulcan, XM651.

prepared, apart from completing the Crew Chief checks and having the systems set to 'Combat' by a spare crew. This meant that they would carry out all the aircrew pre-flight checks on the aircraft, leaving it in a condition as if it were at readiness one-five. This state was known as 'Combat ready' and the crew that carried out the checks, normally comprising a motley collection of 'spare' aircrew, was referred to as the 'Combat Crew'.

As it was now 3 a.m. it was 'dinner time', and so the Chief locked up his aircraft and climbed into his car, departing for the line buildings where transport would be leaving shortly for the Airmen's Mess. This was where the night-time meals for all ranks were served. He never found it short of amazing that a full meal could even be considered at this time of the night, but considered it certainly was, and eaten with relish. Tonight it was turkey with all the trimmings! That night he was accompanied by some of the other Chiefs and the junior engineering officer who was somewhat embarrassed when he was given a whole turkey drumstick to demolish. All he could say when it was finished was, 'Well – we don't get helpings like this at the Officers Mess!'

After the meal and a drink, it was back to his dispersal to await the arrival of his 'Combat Crew' for their checks, and to carry out his own Crew Chief checks. He settled down to look out at the rain that was still falling relentlessly and to wait.

His thoughts drifted back again to the time when he was still new to the job, and to all the extra training he had to carry out. There was the course down at the RAF Aeromedical School, based at North Luffenham in the diminutive County of Rutland, where amongst other things he had been taught the art of 'pressure breathing'. This is mastering the art of breathing oxygen under pressure, which would be necessary if the Vulcan's cabin pressure should fail at altitude. During pressure breathing the whole breathing effort was directed into exhaling and controlling the chest muscles so that the oxygen, which was being fed under pressure through the face mask and into the lungs, did not inflate the chest like a balloon. It was very difficult at first, but with practice it could be easily mastered – sort of breathing back to front. Then there was the decompression chamber where a rapid loss of cabin pressure at altitude was simulated, both with and without oxygen masks. This was not a new experience for the Chief, who had actually experienced an explosive decompression in an Argosy freighter when serving out in the Persian Gulf earlier in his service career – his ear drums had never fully recovered. However this did much to re-assure you that the equipment supplied for your survival did just what it was designed to do and, after all was considered, it made a really interesting break from normal routine.

Then, of course, there were the dinghy drills, mostly held in the local swimming baths, where the skills of righting and manning an over-turned survival dinghy were taught. This was good fun really, but a very essential experience to undergo. However, sometimes this was carried out 'live' in the North Sea and the Chief, not liking water much, was pleased in a way that he had never been involved with one of these seaborne drills!

Perhaps the most exciting of all was the simulator for 'abandon aircraft drills'. This was a nose section of an old Vulcan that was set up on trestles in one of the hangars and was used to familiarise aircrews with drills for abandoning a Vulcan during an emergency. This was very important when a Crew Chief, or even two Crew Chiefs, were carried as crew on overseas exercises. Because of the seating position they occupied within the cabin they had to be the first to abandon the aircraft and if their part went wrong then the survival chances of the rest of the crew members were considerably reduced. This was also the primary reason why Crew Chiefs were not carried at low level as, with five men to get out instead of three, it reduced the chances of survival for the rear crew enormously.

Abandoning an aircraft was a major problem for the rear crew and they always knew that their chances of escape were very slim when the chips were down. It was also decision time for the pilot and co-pilot, who were faced with the knowledge that, with the quick pull of a yellow-and-black striped handle, they could abandon ship quickly and safely, leaving the rear crew to almost certainly perish.

The drill was for the complete crew, sixth and seventh seat members included, who would run through the complete abandonment procedure from the time the 'abandon aircraft' sign illuminated on the rear console.

The seventh seat crew member was first out and as he went he was to slam the emergency operating lever on the door mechanism through its gate, which ensured that the door opened and stayed open under emergency air pressure. The sixth seat member was next, followed by the three rear crew members.

A normal abandonment was deemed to be quite straightforward, and a number of crews had successfully abandoned as such. With the undercarriage down, the escaping crews were confronted with a large, solid metal, nose-undercarriage leg which had to be avoided at all costs. This form of abandonment had never been carried out in practice. The drill was to slide down the door with legs apart, so that your feet straddled the door and stopped on contact with the door opening jacks. You then grasped the starboard door jack with both hands, and swung yourself forcibly and rapidly around the edge of the door and out of the Aircraft. By so doing, you hopefully missed the nose leg whilst being snatched, and propelled towards it by the slipstream! Not much was offered in the way of reassurance for this procedure and I secretly think that the powers-that-be knew very well what the probable outcome would be.

At one time, Martin Baker, the escape systems manufacturer, had devised a means of supplying the rear crew with ejector seats, but this had been turned down simply because it was too expensive.

Of course, there were other hazards to negotiate as the oxygen hose connections for the sixth and seventh seats were not 'snatch disconnect' at this time (they were modified later). If you forgot to disconnect before baling out you were left dangling in the exit chute, suspended by your lead. In the simulator this caused a laugh, but in reality would have spelt certain death for all of the rear crew as, with any loading on it, it was not possible to disconnect the coupling without someone underneath to lift you and relieve the weight. With a dangling man barring the route, escape was denied to all.

The arrival of a crew coach, complete with 'Combat Crew', stirred the Chief from his reflective mood as the captain came into the hut with headset in hand. 'How is it Chief – all hot to trot?' he asked as he looked through the Form 700. 'Yes – no problems at all,' replied the Chief, as they strolled out to the aircraft, pulling the collars of their cold/wet jackets up around their necks against the rain that was falling heavier now and clearing the mist.

The Chief fired up the Diesel 'Houchin' ground power set whilst the crew climbed up the ladder into the cockpit, and then he pulled on his headset, ready for external checks with the crew. This was already connected to his long lead that was coiled and hung over the nose-wheel steering jack.

After their initial cockpit checks a 'Ready control checks' from the crew was responded 'ready' by the Chief, who had now positioned himself about fifty yards behind the bomber, and the sequence of flying control movements was commenced. At each stage the Chief confirmed that the surfaces were moving over full and free movement in the directions prompted by the crew. This was the wettest part of the job when it was raining like this, as for the rest of the checks he would be able to stand under the massive delta wing of the Bomber in a relatively dry environment.

The checks reeled off and the Chief gave his responses from outside with no hitches. Engines were started and after-start checks completed, until a final 'OK Chief, that's about it,' from the captain, as the engines and systems wound down one at a time on completion of the checks. The aircraft was then left at 'Combat ready' for the incoming crew later in the day. This meant that the crew taking over would not need to go through all the checks but would simply get on board the aircraft, fire it up, and go.

The rain still persisted as the Chief tidied up the paperwork. Then he closed and locked the door of his aircraft and, with a final look around, set off for the line building. There he might get another job to complete but hopefully should have a couple of quiet hours before the day shift came in and took over again.

He walked into the building, taking off and shaking his cold/wet jacket, and passed the hatchway through to control. As he did so . . . 'Chief, the Warrant's on Duty Eng. tonight, and down on "Bravo" two-four with a little problem . . . he wants to know whether you can go down and help him out?' came the voice of one of the tradesmen who was manning the control desk to relay messages back and forth.

This referred to his friend, the squadron warrant officer, who was duty engineer that night and had obviously been called out to some incident or other on 'Bravo', the most remote dispersal on the airfield, which was immediately adjacent to the Sleaford Road. A standing joke on the squadron was that if you committed a misdemeanour you would be banished to 'Bravo' dispersal for a week! The Chief thought it was a wind-up at first, but then decided to forego his coffee and left for the car park wondering what on earth his Warrant was up to now.

On nearing 'Bravo' dispersal, he could see that there was a strange looking aircraft, an old one, with four piston engines parked there, possibly a DC7 or something similar . . . he was never very good with recognition of civilian aircraft, but as he drew nearer he could see the faded livery of Icelandic Airways with which it was painted. He could hardly believe his eyes as he took in the scene, being used as he was to highly maintained and spotless warplanes – had this heap of garbage really flown to get here that night? There was oil all over the place, dripping from the engines, which was only partly contained by the drip trays that had been placed there by the RAF personnel to protect the normally spotless concrete dispersal surface. The oil was spreading further by the minute, carried on the film of rainwater that was washing the pan. He could see that some of the inner panels of the double-skinned Perspex windows were broken, with the shattered pieces of plastic slid down into the void between the window skins, and a general air of dilapidation was very much in evidence. The aircrew was not around, but the Chief conjured up the picture of a captain with frayed cuffs and raggy trousers that would exactly match his aircraft! The Chief felt that he had seen better airframes on the station burning-area for the Waddington firemen to practice on!

His friend the Warrant was standing by with an amused smile on his face as the Chief arrived. The Chief thought to himself, 'There must be a big problem here that the Warrant can't handle!' as he had never yet met the situation that this big, affable, and dependable man couldn't handle on his own. He was thinking about their families' cara-vanning days together, when the Warrant took such jobs as the recovery of an itinerant caravan that rolled into the river Nene at Yarwell Mill in his stride – and that was on a weekend away to relax! He also never dreamed that thirty years later he would still be friends with Eric, and actually sitting in his house completing chapter five of his book about the 'good old days'.

'What's up boss?' asked the Crew Chief. 'Come and look at this,' replied the Warrant as he led the way up the steps of the 'Giraffe' that had been positioned at the open freight door of the aircraft, leading into the shabby-looking interior. The odour that hit the Chief reminded him of a farmyard as he noted the row upon row of wooden crates which contained, as far as he could ascertain from the noise, smell, and a rough count – fifty-two horses!

RAF Waddington was officially a 'Master Diversion Airfield', which meant that due to its normally good weather it was guaranteed to be open almost 365 days a year. That signified that any aircraft, military or civilian, could be diverted there in a case of in-flight emergency or bad weather. This aircraft, en route from where to where else heaven only knows, had suffered from what the Chief could see was a not altogether unexpected engine failure. It had diverted to Waddington for what now seemed like a very long stay indeed. The Warrant, in his capacity as duty engineer, had been called out and had put the wheels in motion for the horses to be picked up from the airfield. He also had the job of unloading them first, which proved to be no mean task and so had sent for his friend the Chief to help him out!

Fortunately for the pair, the horses were all in crates and therefore the unloading was accomplished with the use of a fork lift truck from the M.T. section. This was complete with a driver who was none too pleased at being hauled out of bed at that time of the morning, especially in the rain, to cope with what he saw as a 'civvy' problem!

The ensuing transportation of horse boxes, presumably from a local stable, to take the animals away was a long time coming and so the horses had to be watered, which the Warrant and Chief managed between them – from Crew Chief to stablehand in one easy lesson – 'There is certainly variety in this job,' he thought. 'They'll never believe this back home!'

In the aftermath of this incident, the DC7 sat there for a few days awaiting the decision as to what would happen regarding repairs. It transpired that the airline couldn't afford another engine, but at the same time was running up large storage fees at Waddington!

Eventually, after much persuasion and cutting of red tape, the engine fitters of 101 Squadron were approached by the DC7's operating company to work over a weekend and be paid to repair the aircraft, which was then able to be flown off.

Breakfast was very welcome after this long night reached its conclusion. 'Ah well,' he thought, 'there's only another four nights of "Swing" to go before I'll be back on days again.'

The next evening drew on quickly after a good day's sleep and the Chief found that the weather had clamped over the bombing ranges during the day so the sorties were cancelled, and there would be early takeoffs the following day to complete the postponed missions. At midnight, when the Chief came on shift again, he found that there was to be a repeat of the same old merry-go-round, except that this time he would be seeing his aircraft off as well as running through the 'Combats' again (which were valid for twelve hours). Takeoffs were planned for 06.00 in the morning.

On arrival at the dispersal he took over his aircraft from the night shift and, after checking the paperwork, called a status report in to control. It was confirmed to him that the aircraft would be run up by a 'Combat Crew' again that night, to ready it for the early takeoff. He wandered out to the aircraft to make sure that the fuel load was still correct, as further 'Combat' checks had been carried out during that day, which involved starting up the engines, and this would have used yet more fuel. He was right, as the load was several hundred pounds down, so he called for a bowser and refuelling team to top it up, thinking to himself, 'The lazy sods on the night shift could have done that.'

The bowser arrived shortly and he decided to put in just a little more than required, to cater for the forthcoming repeat of 'Combats' and then sent for a servicing team to carry out the before-flight checks.

The before-flight checks were just about complete when the 'Combat Crew' arrived to carry out their procedures. It was a different one from last night, about which the Chief mused, 'I wonder what this lot have done wrong then?'

At least the weather had improved, which was an advantage as they readied the bomber for 'Combats' with the Diesel Houchin roaring into life, emitting a cloud of choking, black smoke as the handler pressed the starter button. Meanwhile the crew climbed into the aircraft to begin their tedious list of checks once more. Control surface movement was proven, with the range of movement indicators in the cockpit being monitored by the crew to ensure that they gave a true indication according to control surface movements relayed to them by the Chief. The pre-start checks were then commenced, with the Chief firing up the 'Palouste' air-starter trolley that would supply the compressed air to turn the engine starter motors.

'Clear one?' queried the captain, to which the Chief responded in the affirmative after running up the Palouste to high rpm, and the captain pressed the starter button for number one engine. 'Light on,' confirmed the captain as the indicator light in the starter button illuminated, telling him that the engine air valve had opened, and the starter air hose stiffened as the air was delivered to the aircraft.

The captain mentally ran through the start up sequence – wait ten seconds – check RPM and oil pressure rising – HP cock towards the idling gate – 8 lb. fuel flow – JPT rising to 350°C – as the engine wound up with a resonating howl to just above idling, to be throttled back as the Chief heard over the intercom, 'Clear two.' 'Clear two,' he responded and the Palouste hose stiffened again as the engine starter turned. 'Light on,' from the captain, and number two wound up to idle, harmonising with number one as the RPM settled. Numbers three and four were then started in quick succession. Soon they were all 'burning and turning' and settled at idle, as the crew ran through their further checks. The Palouste was disconnected, the hose coiled and stowed, and it was pushed behind the safety line at the dispersal edge by the handlers, as the Chief prepared himself for his further checks.

The first task was to check the hot-air trunking at the top front edge of the nosewheel bay, and for this he set up a pair of aluminium steps and climbed up. The Chief was a tall guy, and he only just managed to reach the trunking – heaven knows how the smaller chaps managed to do this job. There were no air leaks evident, which he confirmed to the captain and then he prepared himself for a check of the bomb doors. This was the means by which the functioning of all three hydraulic pumps was checked, as it should take less than eight seconds to open the bomb doors and less than eight seconds to close them. The doors slowly opened and folded on themselves as they moved apart and partly up into the fuselage, exposing as they did so the deadly load of 1,000 lb. bombs, which still had their safety pins and flags attached.

'Less than eight seconds,' noted the captain aloud. 'OK to close Chief?' 'OK to close,' responded the Chief, and the massive doors moved again, relentlessly closing the gap and sealing with a clunk as they finally met. 'Less than eight seconds,' confirmed the captain again, and the Chief acknowledged that all was in order outside.

They ran through the same process in 'emergency power', and then he pulled his ladders clear as the next job was to test the airbrakes. They would be checked at all positions, both in normal and emergency power settings.

'OK air brakes Chief?' asked the captain. 'OK,' replied the Chief, as the large air brakes, two on top and one underneath the engine intake tunnels in each mainplane, moved out. 'Mid,' called the captain, as the brakes stopped at about a foot out. 'Mid,' confirmed the Chief and the brakes started to move again. 'Full,' stated the captain as they stopped and he awaited the reply of 'Full' from the Chief before he selected them to mid again and then to in, with the Chief confirming each movement. The sequence was repeated again in emergency power and when all was confirmed as satisfactory the crew prepared to shut down, which they did, leaving all the cockpit settings at 'Combat'.

It was meal time already and the Chief drove his car to the Mess for yet another early morning feast, which this time turned out to be curry. 'Damn good job I'm not flying with this lot,' he thought humorously as he tucked in to a second helping, remembering the many trips he had made across the pond where the entire crew had to be on 100% oxygen all the way. This was after more than one member had indulged in curry at the Goose Bay Mess in Labrador!

He returned to the line building, where he found that the other Crew

Chiefs had also completed their 'Combats'. At least there were other Crew Chiefs in tonight he thought, for he wouldn't have been able to prepare all six aircraft for the bombing sorties on his own.

However, things never went smoothly and there was a bit of a flap on as one of the primary aircraft had fallen down with a hydraulic snag in one of the undercarriage bays – a door jack had decided to spring a leak after engine start. It would take too long to get a spare from the hydraulic bay and fit it. Anyway, this would have to be a hangar job as independent checks, undercarriage retractions etc, would be needed. Therefore the spare aircraft was being generated and it was 'all hands to the pump'. The Chief grabbed a quick cup of coffee, went out to see what he could do to assist with the preparations and finished up adjusting the fuel load for the incumbent Chief whilst he supervised his before-flight checks and prepared his aircraft for 'Combats'.

Next on the scene were the armourers who had offloaded the 1,000 lb. bombs from the U/S aircraft and were about to load them onto this one, closely followed by the 'Combat' crew, who lounged in the dispersal hut playing cards until the aircraft was finally ready. The dispersal was a frantic hive of activity, but in reality everything was running like clockwork as everyone knew their jobs well, thus ensuring that all would be ready for the planned departure time.

The Chief saw that there was nothing further he could do here to help so he wandered back to the line buildings where he saw with some relief that all preparations were just about complete. He noted that even the controller was in at work now. 'What is it coming to,' he thought, 'when controllers now had to work swing shift!'

The crew room was packed so he went out to his prepared aircraft to await the arrival of the flight crew.

Shortly after arrival on his dispersal, the Hadleigh box squawked at him. 'Yes control,' he replied, depressing the 'talk' lever, 'what is it?' 'We've got the new Junior Eng. in tonight . . . can he come out and watch your crew in?' asked control. There was a new junior engineering officer posted in to the squadron, a young chap straight from university who was very pleasant and whom the Chief liked very much. He certainly had no objections. 'Yes, that's OK . . . make sure that he brings a cold weather jacket and ear defenders though,' he reminded the controller over the box.

The new junior engineering officer arrived with two coffees in his hands, one of which was gratefully received by the Chief, and after a bit of small talk, the Chief explained the sequence of a 'crew in' to him that successfully used up the time until the aircrew arrived.

It was a pleasant surprise when the captain turned out to be the chap that the Chief had just been to the USA and Canada with the previous month. Some animated conversation ensued as they climbed on board to be firmly strapped in, when the captain's and co-pilot's ejection seats were then made 'live'.

The Chief climbed out, and stowed the ladder before closing the door and putting on his headset, which was already singing as the aircraft systems wound up. 'Crew Chief on line captain,' he reported, and after a moments silence, the captain responded, 'OK Chief . . . we'll be starting engines in about five minutes, and then waiting while one and two taxi out before making a move . . . all set out there?' 'All set,' responded the Chief, as the handlers plugged in the Palouste hose again and started the turbine in readiness.

The crew ran through their abridged checks and shortly called, 'Start one'. 'Start one,' responded the Chief, as the engine went through its start sequence and settled at idle. Numbers two and three engines were wound up in sequence with no problems. The captain called, 'Clear four?' 'Clear four,' the Chief confirmed, and once again the palouste hose stiffened as high-pressure air was fed to number four starter motor.

The Palouste seemed to be pumping air for a long time and the Chief was about to ask the crew if they had a problem when the captain came on line. 'Number four won't start Chief, we'll let it wind down and then try again.' 'OK captain,' agreed the Chief, 'tell me when you are ready.' A minute or more elapsed before the captain called again, 'Clear four Chief?' 'Clear four,' he responded and once more the Palouste hose stiffened, this time for an even longer period it seemed, and the Chief was about to tell the captain to shut down when, to his horror, fuel started to pour from number four jet pipe, and splash onto the concrete. 'Stop four!' shouted the chief over the intercom, 'We've got fuel pouring ou . . .' he was cut short as, with a loud 'whooooomff', the fuel ignited in a ball of yellow and red flame, which rose swirling in the night air higher than the tail fin! This rapidly died but the fuel carried on pouring out, bearing the appearance of a fiery waterfall cascading from the jet pipe to the concrete pan surface. It was spreading rapidly over an area about fifteen feet by twelve feet, with the eager flames curling outwards and upwards into the night sky as if seeking out the very structure of the aircraft.

Things happened rapidly now and fortunately the handlers, one of whom was an engine sergeant and new to the squadron, reacted superbly as the new junior engineering officer raced out of the hut with a soda-acid fire extinguisher in his hands running for the blazing spillage of fuel. He was hotly pursued by the engine sergeant who took him down with a rugby tackle halfway across the pan, both coming down with a clump, the fire extinguisher clanking metallically as it tumbled away harmlessly across the pan. 'Thank god for that,' thought the Chief, 'water's the last thing we need on this,' as he and the other handler brought the CO2 bottles to bear on the flames.

It was not an easy task, for no sooner were the flames out on the ground than they were fed by the cascade of still-burning fuel from the jetpipe, which did not seem to be lessening, even though the LP cocks were now shut and all pumps off. The quickly moving aircrew vacated the aircraft, all thoughts of continuing with the morning's sortie somehow driven from their minds.

After the application of a second set of CO2 bottles up the jetpipe at the same time as the first set was played on the burning fuel on the ground, the conflagration was eventually brought under control and then extinguished. The aircrew now reluctantly wandered back to join the Chief, looking at the scorched ground and the fuel still dripping from the jetpipe, as the station fire crews, no doubt having seen the night sky lit up from the other side of the airfield, arrived. This was to the cheers and jeers of the handlers who delighted in informing them that they were too late!

It was only then that they all remembered the twenty-seven live 1,000 lb. bombs which were concealed in the bomb bay, and went weak at the knees as they thought what could have happened on the pan that night had the fire taken hold of the whole airframe.

'What a lot of work for nothing,' thought the Chief as he tidied up his paperwork and went home.

CHAPTER 6

DISPERSAL EXERCISES

It was now the autumn of 1973 and the runways at Waddington were due for resurfacing. This entailed closure of the airfield while it was carried out and so the three Waddington squadrons were detached to operate away from base. Some were detached a few miles down the road to operate out of Scampton while the work was completed. Others were detached further afield to Fairford in Gloucestershire. They would not return until early in 1974. This was a decided inconvenience as, with their living accommodation at Waddington, the return trip to and from Scampton had to be made on most days by the squadron personnel. Travel from and to Scampton took a longer time then than it would today, as it was in the days before the Lincoln bypass was even thought of and all such trips involved passing directly through Lincoln. For the other personnel on the Fairford detachment, weekends were looked forward to as this was the only time that they could spend at home.

Most personnel experienced both detachments, as they were rotated on a regular basis between them, and of the two, the Chief actually preferred the Fairford detachment. The Americans had been at Fairford some time previously and they had a method of refuelling their aircraft that was foreign to RAF personnel at the time. On the aircraft dispersals were refuelling points set in the ground from where the fuel could be drawn to replenish the aircraft without calling for tankers. This system was brought up to speed for the Vulcans and was (in the end) very successful. Initial problems centred around a high water content in the fuel and much testing had to be done. Initially a couple of aircraft were contaminated and had to be drained and flushed, but no operational problems resulted. Shortly into the New Year during 1974, the Vulcans of the Waddington wing were comfortably resettled at their home base and ready for the next phase of their activities. The Fairford personnel were also entertained quite regularly, as the (prototype) Concorde was undergoing much testing and would fly-by quite regularly. Vulcan personnel felt quite an affinity with Concorde, looking upon it as their Vulcan's 'Big Brother'. It was a similar shape, had Olympus development engines, and the Vulcan had been used as a test bed for these.

Due to a new Strike Command directive, aircraft dispersal exercises were now the order of the day. This stated that in the event of an alert being called the Vulcan fleet must be immediately dispersed to several UK airfields as soon as possible, and then further dispersed around the individual airfields. These airfields for the Waddington wing were Wittering, Cottesmore, and Valley. The aircraft were also to be dispersed on each airfield so that if that airfield was the subject of a conventional attack then all aircraft could not be so easily 'taken out' by enemy action.

It never ceased to amuse the Chief that the powers-that-be appeared so naive in their planning. To most service people involved, it was a foregone conclusion that all airfields would be nuclear targets, and not only would all of the Vulcans be taken out in one go, but also the countryside for miles around!

Still, maybe the powers knew something that they didn't and anyway that's the way they wanted it played, and this was going to be practised again and again – ad infinitum, in the very near future. These exercises were known by the code name of 'Kinsman', being exercises with prior notice. Exercises without prior notice were also regularly called and these were known as 'Mickey Finn'. 'Mickey Finns' were a distinct bind from the family's point of view, for you never knew exactly when they were to be called. They could see the point of that, but their families did not know where they would be finishing up or for that matter for how long. This was doubly inconvenient when they did not agree altogether with the thinking behind the strategy in the first place! Still, that fits in with the title of this book very well as they felt that it just went to demonstrate that the V-force, and those who were tasked with operating it, were indeed the proverbial mushrooms of the air force!

Sure enough, on the following Friday an exercise was called at 4 a.m. in the usual manner, by sounding the base siren accompanied by a Land Rover complete with noise-making trailer driving around the camp and married quarters to wake everyone up and summon them into work.

It was usual to have a wash and a shave before you went in – even on an alert – but there were new ground rules now. You had to prove just how fast you could get in and so you literally staggered out of bed, pulled on your trousers and went in to work! A list of arrival times was kept and those persons taking what was considered too long a time to respond were hauled over the coals. It was suggested that they should improve their response times – or else. There was some sense of achievement however, as now that centralised servicing had been well and truly 'thrown out of the window', everyone belonged to their own squadron. If you managed to get things done more quickly than the other outfits, then there was a certain amount of kudos to be earned.

The 101 Line Squadron buildings were buzzing with activity by the time the Chief pulled into the car park, where he quickly found that his next port of call was to the flying clothing section. Here he would pick up his flying kit for a rapid departure in about half an hour for an unknown destination with other Crew Chiefs and groundcrew members who were accompanying a detachment of four Vulcans away to one of the dispersal airfields.

The flying clothing centre was seething with aircrew, all sorting out their kit in one way or another, but it didn't take the Chief long to get his own kit together and report to 'Delta 15' dispersal where his aircraft and crew were already assembled for departure. There was no time for a pre-flight meal today and certainly no knowledge of when they would get their next meal either. It seemed that whatever was in their ration box would have to do them for the foreseeable future.

Equipment and spares were literally being thrown into a 4,000 lb. pannier by the ground crew. This was then secured by the aircrew with a cargo net, and rapidly winched up and secured into the bomb bay. At the same time, a tanker was refuelling the Vulcan, with the aircrew standing around impatiently waiting to start their combat checks as soon as the tanker was clear.

The refuelling was soon completed and the crew climbed in to carry out their combats, only then to find that their status had rapidly changed, and after combat checks were completed, the engines would not be shut down and they were to taxi out and take off straight away. At conclusion of the checks the Chief rapidly coiled his long lead, put it over his shoulder, and after signalling 'chocks away' to the handling team clambered on board, pulling up the ladder behind him and stowing it. The door was raised from inside with a hiss and clunk, and the Chief strapped himself into the sixth seat, feeling very uncomfortable as he was by now streaming with perspiration from his efforts. It was always very confusing at such times – had everything been done, or had something been missed in the panic. Was all his gear strapped on correctly, or would he find out too late, if he had to abandon ship, that some important piece was wrongly connected? Looking around at last and wiping the stinging perspiration from his eyes, he noted in the gloom of the cabin that another Crew Chief was already strapped into the seventh seat opposite him, although he didn't recognise him too well behind his oxygen mask and bonedome. Even as the Chief completed securing and tightening his restrictive straps, they were already taxiing off the dispersal and around to the runway where they became airborne as soon as possible. It seemed that this was accomplished in no time at all and they were climbing away from Waddington in company with another three Vulcans complete with spares panniers and Crew Chiefs, heading for goodness knows where.

Soon, as the sense of urgency subsided amongst the crew and they had calmed somewhat, the destination was made generally known. It was to be RAF Valley in Anglesey, at the north-western tip of Wales. However, they had a high fuel load and this was to be a long trip with a Hi-Lo-Hi sortie carried out on the way. A Hi-Lo-Hi was a sortie where the transit part was carried out at high level, with a couple of 'targets' bombed on the way. If only Sunderland knew how many times its heart had been bombed out by the V-force, they never would have slept so soundly. The aircraft would then descend to low level to attack another simulated target, climbing out to high level again for the return trip. The length of time spent at low level would depend on what sort of mission was being simulated. This was mostly limited by the bombing range size, or length of low-level route over which they were performing. In the UK, most low-level missions seemed to be of short duration because of the lack of wide-open tracts of countryside where low level could be maintained. This was a reason for many of the overseas detachments to places where low level could be flown for many miles. The low level part of this trip was rather bumpy, which made the Chief airsick. 'How droll,' he thought. 'Crew Chiefs weren't supposed to fly on low level missions – until it suited of course, then they would be allowed to do anything!'

Five hours into the trip, and nearing its end, the weather at Valley was reported as starting to clamp in. When they arrived, they only just got down by the skin of their teeth in what amounted to almost zero visibility. No sooner had this been accomplished than the weather clamped in completely, so much so that they had difficulty taxiing through the fog onto their allocated dispersal. In the event, a vehicle was provided, complete with yellow flashing light, to shepherd them at low speed around the airfield and to their parking space. The crew disembarked and climbed onto a crew coach that had arrived to convey them to the mess, whilst the Chiefs fussed around their aircraft and carried out an after-flight inspection. Fuel collector boxes were drained, and ground locks fitted, but no picketing points were available and so they left the hooks stowed on board. The fog seemed to be getting thicker by the minute and was swirling in from the sea like smoke from a fire, and the Vulcan started to drip moisture as the vapour condensed on its metal surfaces. It was eerie, as the sounds normally associated with an airfield were totally suppressed by the blanket of fog, making it feel like they had descended onto another planet entirely. Fuel tankers were then summoned to replenish the nearly empty tanks of the Vulcans and they were 'put to bed' until the next day.

Taking stock of the situation, it was decided that, as visibility was almost zero, the dispersal phase of the exercise, involving moving the Vulcans on the airfield, would be abandoned until the next day when it was hoped that conditions would improve. Therefore the Chiefs retired to the Sergeants' Mess for an unexpected but very welcome stand-down due to the foggy weather.

The usual drinking session in the Mess bar was somewhat subdued that evening, as everyone was tired, and so after a couple of pints or so most retired to bed, as there was an early start planned for the next day.

Dawn arrived all too soon, but the fog was as thick as ever. The day was spent in dispersal huts playing cards and reading some two-month-old newspapers and the odd magazine that had been left behind by the previous incumbents. Movement of aircraft had been totally forbidden on the fog-bound airfield and this seemed to suit everyone, as a growing air of futility about the outcome of this exercise became ever more pervasive. One day of fog lengthened into two days, and then into three. They should have been going home today with the exercise completed, but thankfully there was a better report for tomorrow. However, as tomorrow was Saturday, it was unlikely that they would be flying back to Waddington then. It now looked like they would have to spend the weekend at Valley. 'Fortunately' there was a dance planned at the Sergeants' Mess on Saturday evening and some of them were hoping to go along there, have a few beers, and relax a little. The only problem was that the do was a 'Mess Kit' dinner dance and there they all were, dressed in flying gear complete with boots and not a stick of best dress or even civilian gear between them. Not only that, their kit had been packed for only three days, and by day five things would be getting a little fraught – they were able to recognise their friends from some distance without having to turn around to visually identify them.

Having taken pity on them, the Sergeants' Mess management agreed that they could attend the do, and attend they did with enthusiasm. A lot of beer was consumed, little dancing was done, but they felt that it proved itself to be the highlight of a miserable exercise. One chap who insisted on dancing with one of the local Welsh girls who had been bussed in for the dance, soon abandoned the idea after he had some loud complaints about walking on her toes 'with those bloody great boots!' Another guy, trying to look inconspicuous, borrowed a sports jacket that fitted him around the middle, but had sleeves about six inches too long. He looked even more conspicuous in the end than they did in flying kit!

The next day, Sunday, dawned bright and clear, and so they looked forward to returning to Waddington to get into some clean clothes, but no, this was not to be the case. Just as well perhaps as it is not advisable to fly, especially at low level, with a hangover. If the aircrew had been celebrating in a like manner, then they wouldn't have been able to fly anyway. The 'no drinking' for twenty-four hours before flight was not always observed however, as the Chief could recall one detachment to Goose Bay in Labrador where much merrymaking had taken place. The co-pilot was getting married on his return to the UK, and so everyone had celebrated in style. On the way back from the 'Bulldog Club' where the celebrations had taken place, a group of Crew Chiefs 'lost' one of their number en route. They later retraced their steps to find him passed out and slumped against a lamppost in the sitting position. With temperatures at minus Lord knows what, his clothing had frozen, and he was fixed into an 'L' shape. He was un-ceremoniously hefted onto his heels and slid back, wheelbarrow fashion, to the Sergeants' Mess where he was left in the foyer to thaw out while his compatriots retired to the bar once more.

The next day, everyone had the worst of hangovers and really should not have flown at all, but climb on board they did and zoomed off into the wide blue yonder. The normal practice was for the Crew Chiefs to go onto 100% oxygen – a wonderful hangover cure – and sleep it off during the flight. This was soon accomplished and it was with a sense of eager expectation that the Chief awoke some hours later, looked at his watch, and thought, 'We'll be landing any time at all now.' He soon realised that something was wrong however, as the aircraft noise about him had not changed and it was clear that they were still cruising at altitude. He looked up at the three rear crew members and found that they were all fast asleep. A sense of panic gripped him as he climbed the ladder between the two ejection seats and found that the captain and co-pilot were also fast asleep with the autopilot firmly in control.

Shaking the captain awake, he asked with some urgency, 'Shouldn't we be letting down now – or something?' Suddenly awake, the captain disengaged the autopilot and shouted to the rear crew, 'Come on you lot, where the hell are we?' Rapidly awakening, they were soon fiddling with their gear to find out their current location. The port wing dropped suddenly as the captain wheeled the bomber around on its wingtip onto a reciprocal heading and started to lose altitude rapidly to enter the Waddington approach, which they had somewhat overshot at altitude. A close shave indeed and, had they flown on much further, the incident would have become extremely embarrassing.

Not all incidents were as fraught as that one however, as the Chief could also remember that on one trip, they had taken a young WRAF flying officer along for a 'jolly'. She had flown before, but never in a Vulcan, and as a friend of the co-pilot she was afforded a 'seat' in the 'seventh' position. Now it is true to say that Vulcan bombers do not have the luxury of proper toilet facilities, in fact the arrangements provided are very crude indeed but when the boys are all together who cares. Attachments known as 'pee tubes' are provided and it wasn't long before our WRAF officer passenger wanted to go to the loo! Now, pee tubes are rubber sacks, with a bung in the bottom for draining and a chromed funnel at the top for peeing into. The funnels had tops on them that used to be sprung closed, until some nasty accidents were reported and they were modified to sprung open. Anyway, the lady was handed a pee tube, and she looked at it as if asking, 'How do I use this?' Being too embarrassed, or too polite to really ask properly, she took the tube and retired into the bomb aimer's position, and the crew drew the anti-flash screens across so that she would have some privacy.

She was an awfully long time down there in the depths of the cabin and every now and again a concerned crew member would ask, 'Are you all right in there?' Always came the reply, 'Yes, yes – I'll be out soon!'

When she did come out, it was to be seen that she had an empty pee tube, but was soaking wet all down the legs of her flying suit. When asked what had gone wrong, she held up the blanking plug from the drain end of the pee tube in one hand, the pee tube in the other, and said, 'I just don't know how you manage to get anything through this small hole!'

Back at Valley they soon found that they could look on the dispersal side of the exercise as having only been postponed, and the phase that they considered to have been abandoned would be carried out as planned anyway. They would now be returning to Waddington yet another three days hence if all went well.

Disperse they did, around the airfield, using tugs and towing arms, and after this they sat in draughty dispersal huts for the rest of the exercise. It made a pleasant break really, as the sunshine persisted and, by climbing over the sand dunes adjacent to their dispersal, it was possible to walk along a deserted beach and take their ease. The Red Arrows were stationed at Valley during this period and were equipped with Folland Gnats. This diminutive aircraft was a wonderful flier, and they were entertained daily as they practised their display programme over the airfield. Maybe things weren't as bad as they seemed after all. On Wednesday, they prepared the Vulcans for flight once more, crewed in as normal, and were airborne by mid morning. You guessed it – another Hi-Lo-Hi sortie was completed, but this time the Chief managed to keep his breakfast down, and by 3 p.m. we were in the circuit at Waddington – another mind-blowing exercise completed.

It was nice to have a bath and get into some clean clothes, and even to get settled back into the usual work routine. After a while though, this became tedious as, although we 'hated' exercises, we got so used to this way of life – it was boring without them. They didn't have to wait long, for soon another Kinsman dispersal exercise was called at 10 p.m. one evening and they were off again.

This time the exercise was not too far away from Waddington, only a short distance down the A1 at Wittering, now known as 'The Home of the Harrier'. They were going there by road this time, letting the Vulcans find their own way there after the Hi-Lo-Hi sortie that now seemed the norm for dispersal exercises. The Crew Chiefs and handlers would be going today, followed by the Vulcans tomorrow.

Wittering was without aircraft of its own at this time, and one of their first tasks was to traverse the main runway and ensure that it was free of debris to accept the Vulcans on their arrival. A spin along its length soon showed up a rather serious problem. There had been a recent heatwave and as the runway was fabricated from concrete blocks about twelve feet square, they had suffered expansion, and two of them had risen pyramid fashion by twelve inches making it impossible to land over them. Fortunately this was to the north side of the runway threshold and so, after an amount of deliberation, it was decided to land the Vulcans anyway, but keep them south of the runway centreline.

The Vulcans landed without incident, and they dispersed them around the airfield as required. One of them had landed with an ECM unserviceability and was having one of its ECM cans, which were mounted in the appendage aft of the fin and rudder, replaced. Unfortunately, there was rather a high wind blowing, and this caught one of the large doors that had to be swung down to change a can, bent it back on its hinges, and the door was badly damaged. A new door was sent down from Waddington and it was fitted to the Vulcan overnight on the dispersal. This was no mean feat, as with the wind still blowing, the door was very hard to hold, and a windbreak of fuel tankers and three-ton trucks had to be driven into position around it. Even then it took several hours to remove the old door and fit a new one. Ah – the pleasures of working in the field!

This detachment proceeded without further incident and, at the end of it, the Vulcans took off with their customary scramble, and the groundcrew and Crew Chiefs packed up the spares to make their way home.

The spares were not transported with them for, as Wittering was one of the recognised dispersal airfields, a row of lock-up garages was at their disposal and it was there that everything was held. On a regular basis it would be checked and replenished. Such things as nitrogen replenishment trolleys and rapid air-bottles would lose pressure and need replacing. There was nothing worse than to find that someone had not done their job properly and everything was flat!

As is usual on such detachments, they always tried to leave their mark in some fashion on the hosting station, and this time was no exception. It was the period when the IRA threat was building in mainland Britain, and security was the watchword. At the gates of Wittering, they had an armed guard and he inhabited a large sentry box complete with telephone.

On their way out of camp, in a three-ton truck, they stopped and told the guard that they were the station warrant officer's working party, and had come to take his sentry box in for painting. He was most co-operative, and laying his rifle on the ground, he helped them to disconnect his telephone, and load the box into the back of the three-tonner. Back they drove with it to Waddington.

It was placed on the 101 Squadron car park at 'Echo' dispersal, as it was there that the squadron warrant officer stood to catch latecomers in the mornings. There were many 'dodges' employed by people to thwart his attentions, but he sussed them all, and the worst offenders were found to be senior NCOs. One Crew Chief thought he had the dodge to end all dodges. He would come in to work an hour late in his overalls, with his long lead slung over his shoulder, and headset clamped around his neck. He would stroll in as though he was coming in from a job. He was eventually caught, and suffered some dire consequences.

On a regular basis, the Crew Chiefs used to gather in the Warrant's

XH558 parked in the Waddington hangar on 10 August 1992.

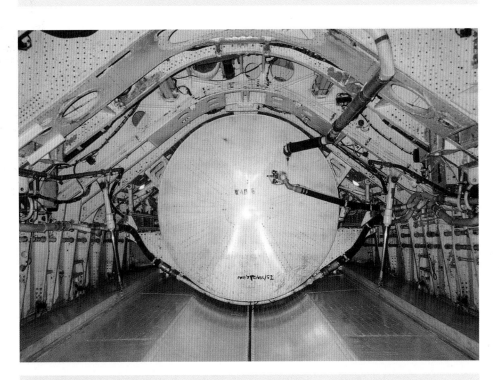

The business end of a Vulcan bomber – the cavernous bomb bay that will carry twenty-one 1,000 pound iron bombs.

Vulcan XH558 at Waddington on 28 April 1990.

XH558 at Waddington.

XH558 approaches over the Grantham road at Waddington, 23 February 1993.

Vulcan XH558 taxies in front of the AWACS at Waddington.

XH558 taxies at Bruntingthorpe with its tail 'chute still attached on 23 March 1993

A Crew Chief's eye view of the 'top floor' when standing on the ladder between the seats.

XJ825 meets her undignified end at Waddington in 1992 as she falls foul of the scrapman's JCBs.

office of a morning to be allocated their jobs, and it was there they were gathered with coffee when he came in from the car park – more than a little bemused. 'There's a sentry box on the car park,' he stated in his well-known Geordie brogue, 'What the 'ell's that there for?'

'Ha!' stated a big Scots Crew Chief, (the same guy that was frozen into an 'L' shape at Goose Bay), 'That's so's you won't get wet when it rains.'

After the laughter subsided, the Warrant could see the funny side of it and he actually inhabited the box for the next couple of mornings. It didn't take long for the s**t to hit the fan, so to speak. Wittering traced their sentry box, and it had to be returned forthwith. There didn't appear to be any flak flying about after it either.

After a while, the need for dispersal exercises seemed to fade, and life got back to normal, with just the occasional 'Taceval' (Tactical Evaluation) exercise being called. This was a replacement for Kinsman and Mickey Finn, and involved a team of umpires visiting the station. They would arrive out of nowhere, call the Taceval and would then monitor all aspects of it thereafter. It may or may not have finished up with a scramble and dispersal, but most often it was simply terminated after two or three days. It involved a lot more play acting than the earlier exercises did. If personnel were in the Mess for lunch when a gas attack occurred (shouts of, 'Gas, gas, gas', accompanied by the donning of gas masks) or a fallout warning was posted (NBC suits on quickly), they had to stay there for the duration.

One weekend, a 101 Squadron open day was arranged, to provide a day out for the families. This was staged at 'Echo' dispersal and a large crowd of dependants gathered to see what their husbands, sons, and daughters all did for a living, and to watch a flying display that was being staged especially for them. There were also a number of visiting aircraft, and amongst these was a Lightning fighter. This is mentioned only because it happened that the same 'A Tech' who blew down the 'Echo' dispersal garages during an unauthorised engine run managed to discharge its fire extinguishers whilst it was parked on dispersal.

A Vulcan had taken off some time earlier to put on a display somewhere or other with a fuel load of only 20%. When he got back to Waddington, he was going to be putting on a special display for everyone at the 101 Squadron open day – with nearly empty tanks! Needless to say, if it is related that the captain was no less a personage than Sqn Ldr Joe L'Estrange, you can reason just how good a display it really was. The Chief could honestly say that in all his time of involvement with Vulcans he had never seen flying like this. The most amazing display that he had ever seen was carried out, and all within the bounds of the 'H' plan of dispersals that formed the 'Echo' complex. He had never smelt the burnt fuel from an airborne aircraft before, nor been able to count the rivets, or ever felt the slipstream as it flew by – he did this time! After a buffet meal and a tour around the visiting aircraft, it was time to go home after a most memorable day.

CHAPTER 7

CHANGING FORTUNES: A SUNFLOWER THAT WASN'T

It was October 1975, and Vulcan XM645 took off for Malta with a full crew including two Crew Chiefs, one of whom was a friend of the Chief, having attended the same ASC course during 1969. It was well remembered how they had many nights out in the Sergeants' Mess bar, especially the 'passing out night' at RAF Newton, where a considerable amount of ale was consumed by everyone. It finished up with the Chief's friend taking an early (?) night and falling asleep on his bed immediately. The others all carried him, in his bed, out onto the sports field and covered him up with grass clippings. He spent the night out there, waking up in the morning and wondering where on earth he was. Happy memories of happier days.

The other Chief on board was a new Crew Chief on his first familiarisation sortie. Everything went well until, when making a practice overshoot at Luqa, they undershot the runway, coming down very heavily in the undershoot area. So heavily, in fact, that the undercarriage was driven up through the mainplane and, soon on fire, the aircraft became very difficult to control. The captain tried desperately to get some height on so that his rear crew could escape, but by now, with ruptured fuel tanks, the conflagration had developed to an extent where the bomber was no longer controllable. The top crew were left with no option but to declare an 'abandon aircraft', and shortly thereafter ejected to safety. Unfortunately the rear crew, together with both Crew Chiefs, was not so fortunate and all perished in the subsequent crash. Large pieces of the aircraft fell in a populated area, over the village of Zabbar, and a woman was also killed on the ground and several others injured. Most of the street and houses were also burnt out. This was an incident that has never been forgotten in Malta, and there is to this day a museum of crash wreckage and a shrine to remember the dead in the village of Zabbar. The bodies of the aircrew were all brought back to the UK and the Chief can well remember the funeral of his friend at Lincoln Crematorium, where he was a pall-bearer.

Time had now moved on to late December 1975; Christmas had passed sorrowfully, but peacefully, and with a Sunflower Ranger coming up before the new year, the Chief had a lot of planning to do. He had also to assemble a schedule of spares to take halfway around the world with him in a 4,000 lb. pannier that would be fitted into the bomb bay of his Vulcan.

This would have to sustain him for all eventualities and would contain things such as spare main and nose wheels, spare brake units, radio sets, NBS boxes, and all manner of items that were notorious for breaking down at inconvenient times and places. He would also take a spare tail braking parachute with him as this could save him a very tedious repackaging job if the crew decided to stream the 'chute that was fitted during landing.

He would also have to find out which aircraft had been selected for the exercise and double check that the planners in central engineering control had done their job correctly in assessing the hours available for the duration of the trip. There were items such as S.I.s (Servicing Instructions), which had to be carried out at intervals, to be considered and S.T.I.s (Special Technical Instructions) that had to be actioned within so many flying hours of their issue. The hours left to the next check servicing would have to be reviewed and if the aircraft needed more hours than it had left to complete the trip then this was usually granted as an extension by the senior engineering officer on the station.

He also had to get his 'jabs' up to date and his passport must be checked; not that he would need it, as it had never been required wherever he went. However, rules were rules and 'Sod's law' dictated that he would certainly be asked to produce it if ever it was forgotten.

He was actually taking his own aircraft, XM651, on this trip with him and that made a pleasant change, for Crew Chiefs developed an affinity with their own bombers in time but seldom got to fly away with them. It was actually a 44 Squadron show and XM651 was from 101 Squadron, but for trips like this aircraft were selected in accordance with hours to go before servicing etc. and they were often swapped between squadrons. This was different to the old days when the Vulcan was tasked as the main nuclear deterrent for the United Kingdom. Then each aircraft had two Crew Chiefs who stayed with it

Opposite: The report of the crash of XM645 in Malta taken from the *Times of Malta* where the Chief lost a good friend.

TIMES OF MALTA

No. 12,464　　　　WEDNESDAY, OCTOBER 15, 1975　　　　Price 3c

SIX DEAD, 20 INJURED AS RAF VULCAN CRASHES AT ZABBAR

By Our Staff Reporters

Tragedy hit the Royal Air Force and the people of Zabbar simultaneously yesterday at lunchtime. A giant Royal Air Force bomber, a "Vulcan", arriving from Britain on an exercise flight, exploded in mid-air as it was making its landing approach over Zabbar.

Five of its seven-men crew were killed as was a woman who was walking up Sanctuary Street, the main street of the village. About 20 other people were injured, some seriously. One of them, a boy named Kevin Falzon, was hit by a falling fragment and was later operated upon at St. Luke's Hospital.

Two members of the aircraft crew ejected safely and descended by parachute. They were taken to Mtarfa hospital for treatment to slight injuries. The names of the dead crew members were not disclosed yesterday pending notification of the next of kin. The woman, said to be a resident of Zabbar, was not identified up to late last night.

A Royal Air Force spokesman said that the "Vulcan" was making its approach landing after flying from the United Kingdom on a training flight. It carried no weapons.

The spokesman confirmed that the aircraft carried a crew of seven. Two of them ejected and were taken to Mtarfa Royal Naval Hospital. The other five are unaccounted for.

People witness explosion

It was a tragedy seen happening by thousands of people in widely separated parts of the island. The majority were agreed

The wreckage of the "Vulcan" bomber in a field at Zabbar. Fire-fighters from the R.A.F. and the Royal Navy, assisted by men from the Armed Forces of Malta, Admiralty Constabulary, the Police and civilians are pictured searching among the wreckage and connecting fire pumps. More pictures on Page 13.

on two things: that the plane was on fire before the explosion and that it came down in three large pieces.

The largest piece, which included at least three of the engines and part of the undercarriage, fell in a small field surrounded by carob trees at the edge of the village and very close to the Government Primary School. This part burned fiercely for some time, beating back would-be rescuers of the crew members said to have been trapped in the plane.

Rescue squads demolished a wall to make way for the crash tenders which sped all the way

(Cont. on Page 3)

Eye-witnesses' accounts

One of the people nearest the scene of the crash was Mrs. Tessie Zlafa, a mother of seven children. Her house, in Carmel Street, overlooks the field where the biggest part of the fuselage fell.

Mrs. Refalo said she was on the roof, feeding three of her children. I saw the plane coming in. It was wrong. Then it exploded and broke into three big pieces and several other small ones.

"I gathered my children and rushed downstairs. Then there

was a terrific noise. I did not see it crash in the field. We certainly had a lucky escape particularly since the house shook badly"

Mrs. Manwela Zerafa heard a loud explosion and ran outside. "I thought it was an earthquake. Then I saw a blinding flash and the whole street appeared to go up in flames. I heard screams as the flames rushed along the street and the shop (meaning the one opposite her house) started burning.

Mrs. Emmanuela Caruana, whose house was damaged by the flames, said she looked up on hearing an explosion and saw the plane break up and begin to come down in flames. "I rushed inside hoping that the plane would not hit the house", she said. It did not, but one piece fell close to the house "and then there was a big fire", she said.

Several people spoke highly of the headteachers at the Secondary, Primary and Boys Schools. They first took all the children inside, then when things quietened down they sent them

WEATHER

The following were yesterday's Fahrenheit noon temperatures:

Cairo	68 sunny
Hongkong	71 slurmy
London	48 cloudy
Malta	
Melbourne	59 cloudy
Perth	68 cloudy
Rome	60 rainy
Singapore	87 sunny
Sydney	72 sunny
Tokyo	67 cloudy

Political crisis in Australia

(Reuter's Service)　　　　CANBERRA, Oct. 14

Australia's Labour Government today faced political crisis and the possibility of being forced into elections over a secret attempt to raise up to 8,000 million U.S. dollars in Middle East oil money for development loans.

The affair forced the resignation today of Minerals and Energy Minister Rex Connor, one of the most powerful figures in the Cabinet.

It could also produce a constitutional crisis if the Opposition chooses to break with tradition and force elections by blocking budget legislation in the Senate, normally a review chamber.

The burly, 18-stone Mr. Connor, 68, was forced to quit the Cabinet when a London-based financier disclosed alleged secret communications on an oil-fund swoon.

Prime Minister Gough Whitlam told Parliament he had been misled by Mr. Connor and had asked for his resignation. He named Senator Ken Wriedt, the Agriculture Minister, to take over Mr. Connor's portfolio.

Mr. Connor was the second prominent figure forced out of the Cabinet by the Middle East loan question since it came to light in the *(cont. Backpage Col. 3)*

Portuguese Army Chief of Staff in Oporto

(Reuter's Service)

LISBON, Oct. 14.

The Portuguese Army Chief, General Carlos Fabiao, travelled today to the northern city of Oporto where rebellious Leftist soldiers have occupied the local Artillery barracks for more than a week.

The occupation has become a symbol both of Left Wing opposition to the Government and of the Government's determination to restore military discipline.

A red flag flew over the barracks today as local workers waited to see how General Fabiao dealt with the continuing rebellion.

The General's trip followed a warning from Prime Minister Jose Pinheiro de Azevedo that military unrest threatened his Government's existence.

Leftist backed insubordination spreading through the ranks of the armed forces undermined

Kidnapped Dutch businessman may be alive

(Reuter's Service)

DUBLIN, Oct. 14.

Dutch businessman Dr. Tiede Herrema's kidnappers have indicated in a new message that he is still alive, and named a new negotiator to replace Capuchin Friar Donal O'Mahony, it was stated here today.

The local Government and Public Services Union said in a statement that its Deputy General Secretary, Mr. Philip Flynn, had been named in the message as the new mediator.

"It is clear from it that Dr. Herrema is alive and that further speculation in this regard is unhelpful," the Union said.

It was the first word from the kidnappers, believed to have broken away from the Irish Republican Army (I.R.A.) since last Thursday and fears had grown that Herrema was dead.

The 54-year-old head of the Dutch-owned Ferenka Tyre components factory was abducted near his Limerick home 11 days ago.

MOSCOW, Oct. 14

French President Valery Giscard d'Estaing opened talks with Soviet Communist party leader Leonid Brezhnev in the Kremlin, two and a half hours after flying in on a five day official visit today.

The two leaders made ceremonial entries from opposite ends of the white and gold painted Saint Catherine's Hall in the Kremlin's grand palace where the talks are being held.

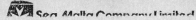

streets all too narrow and jammed by people who rushed to the scene of the accident.

Woman's death

The piece which did the most damage and caused the death of the woman and the injury to other persons, was the one that fell in Sanctuary Street. Obviously the part of the aircraft containing the fuel tanks, it exploded on impact with the ground, sending a searing wall of flame, two storeys high down the street, away from the Parish Church.

The right hand side of the street, going down from the parish church, was blackened by the flames. Wooden balconies and window frames were burned out. Part of a building was demolished and cars were burned over a hundred houses and shops suffered considerable damage.

On the pavement lay the blackened, burnt body of an old woman, her shopping bag near her.

A bread van, standing in the street, was completely burned out. Its owner-driver is said to have run away immediately he saw the piece of plane hitting the ground, then bravely returned to render assistance to whoever needed it. Nearby lay a Cortina, a Renault and a Triumph car all completely gutted. A "Datsun" car, parked on the opposite side of the road, had one side completely burned out.

Honeymooners' lucky escape

The "Triumph" belonged to a couple from Wales who are hon come from Cardiff and Barry, were on their way for a swim at St. Thomas Bay. They had one of the luckiest escapes.

"We saw a ball of fire and then a huge portion of the wing coming towards us. It was horrifying," they said. They abandoned their car and managed to run away from the searing flames. Within seconds the car was just one blaze.

The third part of the aircraft fell on a garage where buses are parked at night. It hung incongruously on the edge of the building, right in front of the Government primary school. Another part fell in a field close by, where the school building, while other parts fell on nearby buildings.

Scenes of panic

The crash sent the people into a panic. Women, some weeping, others screaming, left their houses and ran as fast as they could away from the wreckage. Many ran towards the school where about 200 children were gathered before beginning their afternoon lessons. Others went to the playground close by, where children were playing. Happily none of them was hurt.

The panic was followed by another, as many husbands left their place of work and rushed to Zabbar by the first means of transport available to enquire about their families and relatives. This proved more difficult than ever, particularly since people near the disaster area had evacuated their homes and the police cordoned off the area letting no one to approach the houses some of which were burning at the time.

The rescuers

Rescue and fire-fighting operations were mounted at once. From R.A.F. Luqa came a steam of crash tenders, fire engines, ambulances and mobile cranes. Sirens blazing, they raced to the area of the crash, their progress hampered by the narrow streets, haphazardly parked vehicles and thick crowds all making their way to the scene of the crash. When they got there, they found a mass of burning wreckage.

For the airmen trapped inside the plane there was no hope. The twisted, charred and unrecognizable wreckage made it impossible for anyone to remain alive. The rescue and fire-fighting crews were hemmed in by sight seers who simply would not obey the orders of the police or the hundreds of R.A.F. personnel who cordoned off the area for rescue purposes and to keep away souvenir hunters.

The rescuers suffered from lack of water. Having exhausted both the foam and the water carried in the tenders, they desperately sought a well in the vicinity. They only succeeded after a long time. For hours after the crash, the fire-fighting tenders ran a shuttle service to and from the scene of the crash, filling up and leaving only to return after again filling up.

The Commando carrier "Hermes", moored in Grand Harbour, sent up her helicopters. One a "Sea King" landed in a field. From it came out rescue crews and ambulance men. Two other helicopters, "Wessexes", also flew to the scene bringing more rescue personnel. The Malta Armed Forces "Frelon"

Energy Ministerial Conference

PARIS, Oct. 14.
New problems emerged today as the world's leading non-Communist oil producing and consuming countries met here to finalize plans for a full-scale Ministerial conference, informed sources said.

But the difficulties would not wreck the chances of the Ministerial conference opening here on December 16 as scheduled, the sources said.

The conference is expected to lay the foundations of a new international economic order tionally, worked hard both in the rescue and fire-fighting and in helping to keep the roads clear of sightseers and vehicles. Numerous ambulances, Government, R.A.F. and Royal Navy and even one from the St. John Ambulance Brigade, were on the scene.

The Police worked alongside the rescuers helping them in more ways than one. Their biggest task was to clear people away from the wreckage. Royal Marine Commandos from 41 Commando Group R.N. brought rescue equipment and more water.

Naval, R.A.F. and civil government doctors and nurses stood by to help the injured.

The President Sir Anthony Mamo and the Prime Minister, Mr. Mintoff, were on the scene of the crash shortly after the accident happened. Also present were Dr. A. Buttigieg, Deputy Prime Minister, Miss A. Barbara, Minister of Labour, Employment and Welfare, Dr. A. Hyzler, Minister of panicked by Mr. L. Sant, Minister of Public Building and Works, also visited the scene of the crash. Mr. Haydon expressed his condolences and sympathy to the people. Through the Office of the Prime Minister, Mr. Haydon also expressed his sympathies and condolences to the people of Malta.

The Department of Information said yesterday that following assurances from the R.A.F. and Government architects that there was no danger to the primary and secondary schools at Zabbar, parents should send their children to school as usual today.

A full scale inquiry into the circumstances is expected to be held by the Royal Air Force. It is likely that a special investigating team will be flown out from Britain immediately to carry out the investigation. A search is expected to start for the black box, the instrument which could well tell the investigators the reasons for the crash.

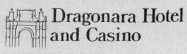

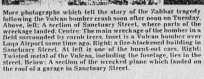

More photographs which tell the story of the Zabbar tragedy following the Vulcan bomber crash soon after noon on Tuesday. Above, left: A section of Sanctuary Street, where parts of the wreckage landed. Centre: The main wreckage of the bomber in a field surrounded by carob trees. Inset is a Vulcan bomber over Luqa Airport some time ago. Right: a fire-blackened building in Sanctuary Street. At left is one of the burnt-out cars. Right: Twisted metal of the Vulcan, including the fuselage, lies in the street. Below: A section of the wrecked plane which landed on the roof of a garage in Sanctuary Street.

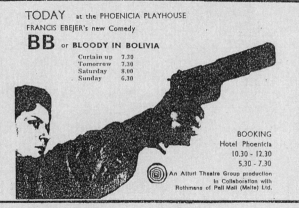

through thick and thin. The Chiefs even took their bomber into the hangar and accompanied it to St Athan or Woodford where the major servicing or 'Check Fives' were carried out.

QRA was also different then as it was carried out a week at a time and the Chief was an integral part of the crew for that period.

Of course, now the Crew Chiefs on a squadron were all in a 'pool' and possessed an aircraft as an inventory item only, which was a much better scheme all round. The only trouble was that it was very hard to keep track of your inventory sometimes as someone else always seemed to be away with it.

XM651 was a very good aircraft, maintaining an excellent service-ability record, and that was good as it meant that running-spares requirements could be predicted with some certainty and the amount of components taken along 'for luck' could be kept to a minimum. This meant a bit of spare room in the pannier for taking along things such as the Chief's push bike, which had more than proved its worth when the Vulcan was parked at the furthest extreme of a foreign airfield.

There would also be plenty of room in the pannier for bringing back lots of goodies and the duty-frees for the whole crew! This was one trip that he could look forward to.

The Chief was also pleased that XM651 was going with him this time as it now sported some rather smart livery in the form of a 'Magpie' badge on the crew entrance door. Magpie was a popular children's TV programme at the time and they had adopted a Vulcan as a part of their presentation. The Squadron CO had been nominated as crew captain, along with the Chief who normally accompanied him, and wherever they went postcards would be sent back to the programme to be read out by the presenter, Susan Stranks, on TV. Viewers were continually updated as to what XM651 and its crew were up to and in what part of the world they were operating. Magpie badges were sported on flying suits and this raised eyebrows wherever they went.

All seemed well with the aircraft preparation, so the Chief arranged for the spares he required to be lashed into a pannier in one of the dispersal garages, ready to be loaded to XM651 on the next day, as on the following day they would be flying off.

Everything went smoothly and after checking around the aircraft the Chief decided that he would prefer the starboard front outer main-wheel to be changed as he felt that it would need replacing too soon into the exercise thus lowering his spares capability. He also packed a couple of 'SOAP' and magnetic plug kits for the engines as these items would need sampling and checking respectively at intervals whilst he was away.

The flying suit patch worn by the Chief during the time that XM651 was associated with the Magpie kids' TV programme.

'SOAP' was an abbreviation for 'Spectrometric Oil Analysis Programme', which involved taking a small engine oil sample which was then sent away for a technical analysis. This would identify the types and quantities of metals suspended in the oil that were worn off bearings etc. The amount and type of metal then gave clues as to the rate of wear on the engine, indicating if there was anything out of the ordinary happening that would need further investigation, which usually involved an engine change. The magnetic plugs, which were situated in various engine oil sump positions, were also a reliable indicator of anything breaking up inside the engine and gearboxes. These also were removed at intervals and sent for analysis. He would need OX 38 engine oil, a lot of it, as the Olympus engines were notorious for consuming oil and it was not uncommon for some engines to use nearly a pint an hour. This could mean a top up of up to fifteen or even twenty pints on all four after a five-hour trip. As they could clock up twenty-five flying hours or more on a trip like this he decided to take along fifteen gallons on the assumption that there wouldn't be any available en route. Hydraulic oil was another requirement, and it was losses during replacements of components that had to be catered for here, so in went six gallons of OM 15 as well for good measure. After all, everything could be brought back if it was not used, but get stuck somewhere for a gallon of oil and there would be hell to pay!

The pannier was just about loaded now, so the Chief decided to call it a day and retire to the Mess for a meal and an early night, as it was up with the lark tomorrow for final preparations and a meet with the aircrew for a tactical discussion.

The TV news that night was not good and, as usual, there was a war going on somewhere in the world. This time it was Cyprus, as the Turkish army had invaded their shores in mid-1974 and had occupied the north end of the island. The two resident Vulcan squadrons had been quickly withdrawn to Malta, eventually to be transferred to the UK. 35 Squadron had gone to Scampton, and 9 Squadron had come to Waddington.

The next morning, after breakfast, he made his way to the aircrew rest room in the hangar for a cuppa with his crew and a discussion about the Sunflower itinerary. As he approached the crew room it was plain to see that there was something unusual afoot, as it seemed as if the entire aircrew of the squadron was there at the same time.

He saw his captain by the tea bar and joined him, asking, 'What's happened boss, why is everyone rushing about?'

'It looks like the Sunflower's on hold Chief, things have really blown up in Cyprus and it looks like we've got to get out there and show the flag,' replied the captain resignedly. It seemed like the southern sector of Cyprus that supported a large population of British ex-pat civilian personnel was also now in danger, and it had been decided to reinforce the military presence there by sending out four Vulcans on exercise 'Forearm'.

The Chief's spirits sank immediately as he realised that the Sunflower that he had been looking forward to was now decidedly 'out of the window', and his plans would have to be drastically revised. 'When are we going?' he asked, to be told by his Captain, 'Yesterday! . . . No, actually we're the only ones ready, so we're going today and three more aircraft will follow us tomorrow. You'd better get that pannier onto the aircraft straight away and we'll see you at the aircrew diner at 16.00 hours – all kitted up and ready to go Chief!'

The Chief rushed from the squadron hangar back to the Sergeants' Mess to finish packing – it was a good job he had almost finished it earlier as he would also need to revise what he was taking along. He managed to phone up flight safety to order his parachute etc. and took all his kit over to the squadron garages and packed it in the pannier just before the groundcrew arrived to take it out to the aircraft. The Chief went with them, sitting aboard the pannier as it was towed to the dispersal, and then supervised its loading to the aircraft. The minihoists were hooked to brackets on the bomb arches and the weighty pannier was then winched into position and secured. Then the minihoists were removed and stowed on the sides of the pannier and the bomb doors closed. The Chief handed the aircraft over to another Crew Chief who would do the rest of the flight preparation for him, enabling him to climb on board when the departure time arrived together with the crew.

After all the messing about during the morning it was already lunch time, so the Chief made his way to the Sergeants' Mess making a pact with himself of 'no curry today' in deference to the long flight ahead. Instead he settled for roast beef followed by apple pie for sweet and, after a sit down to digest his meal and relax, it was off to the flying clothing section to collect his kit.

The Chiefs all had their own lockers in the flying clothing section where they stowed certain 'personal issue' items of flying clothing such as cloth helmets, oxygen masks, flying suits etc., which he picked up. Then he went to the counter for issue of his parachute and survival pack. The survival pack would be his seat for five hours and the parachute would be his uncomfortable backrest as they were both to be worn at all times whilst airborne.

All his kit was loaded into his car and driven around the airfield to XM651's dispersal where he stowed it on board, with the exception of his flying suit which he now wore over the green sweatshirt that was current aircrew issue. Getting rid of his flying kit in this manner enabled him to park his car at the Sergeants' Mess and walk over to the aircrew diner. He was about an hour early, but that gave him time to relax a little with the flight safety magazines in the foyer and await his crew for the pre-flight meal. This was always a substantial meal and they would have to make the most of it in this instance, for flying into a situation such as existed in Cyprus at this time you never knew when your next meal would be.

'Hi Chief,' greeted the captain as he walked in the door, followed by the rest of the crew, 'All fit?'

'Yes, everything's done, but you'll have to stow your kit in the bomb aimer's position as the pannier's full now,' replied the Chief.

'No problem,' said the captain airily, 'have you got a cargo net for it?' The captain referred to the practice of putting a cargo net over luggage that was carried on the floor in the bomb aimer's position to lash it securely down.

'Yes, that's all out there waiting,' responded the Chief as he rose from his seat and followed them into the dining room.

The atmosphere was usually light hearted during pre-flight meals, where the Chief could renew acquaintances with crew members he had not seen for some time, and he was pleasantly surprised to find that another Crew Chief was coming along as seventh seat member. It always made the trip more agreeable when the Chief had another Crew Chief along as not only did it halve his work load but it meant that he had somebody along that he knew when booking into a strange Sergeants' Mess while the aircrew departed to the Officers' Mess. On some exercises the crew had to remain integral however, and this meant that the Crew Chiefs would live and eat at the Officers' Mess also, but not on this trip.

All too soon the meal was over, signalled by the arrival of a coach to take them out to XM651 to prepare for departure. The Form 700 was signed up and the travelling Form 700A was taken on board by the Chief as, for obvious reasons, the main document was not allowed to fly with its own aircraft. They could hear that power was already running on the prepared aircraft as they walked out and with a last look around they ascended the ladder from the sunshine into the dark and cramped interior of the cabin.

Once on board time almost ceased to exist as there was so much to do before takeoff and the Chiefs busied themselves by strapping into their heavy and cumbersome gear. The survival pack hung under their bottoms, secured by webbing straps to the parachute, which had its own restricting harness to encompass and further restrict the body. On top of all this, when it was time for takeoff, the webbing straps of the 'seat' harnesses followed. It was not too bad wearing all this gear when you were sitting down in your 'seat', which was in reality a wooden platform with a harness assembly mounted onto a metal frame behind it that was secured to the aircraft structure using 'pip' pins. Indeed, the guy who designed this seat must have thought that Crew Chiefs were natural contortionists and the seventh seat position was even worse – the Chief was glad that he was not sitting there on this flight.

With the aircraft being 'Combat ready' it was not necessary to run through all the normal crew-in checks and it was sufficient for normal pre-start checks to be carried out before the engines were fired up and the taxi and takeoff completed.

The engines were started using a Palouste turbine starter to conserve rapid air and then, with a parting word of thanks to the Crew Chief outside, the throttles were blipped to 40% or so to 'unstick' the Aircraft from the pan. Then it was simply a matter of following the directions of the handler who was marshalling them out of the dispersal and onto the taxiway. With a final parting wave from the captain to the handler they were on their way.

The Vulcan taxied easily under the idling thrust from all four engines, in fact it was difficult to keep the speed down without the use of gentle braking, and they were soon lined up on the runway threshold with brakes applied and reeling off the pre-takeoff checks.

The checks progressed rapidly, brakes applied – open throttles to 80% – check stabilisation – airframe anti-icing on – parking brake off – main brakes released – throttles open to full thrust, and with a seemingly irresistible heave of power, the Vulcan's nose rose slightly and it began to move down the runway. As it did so, the roar of the engines characteristically flattened out with the intake resonance projecting the unmistakable howl of the Olympus 301 powerplants. A massive 80,000 lb. of thrust cleaved the air behind like a deranged tornado as the Vulcan accelerated along the runway. The Chiefs and the other rear-facing crew members were pushed, as if with a great hand, against the restraint of their harnesses, feeling almost as if they would be left behind. The captain and co-pilot were also forced against their seat equipment by the mounting 'G' force of accelera-tion. The detachment you felt inside the Vulcan at a time like this seemed strange as the engines could be heard but somehow felt abstracted and part of a performance that was being played out far away.

The co-pilot reeled off the relevant information: – 60 knots – rudder now effective, 100 knots – 120 – 140 – 160 – V1, rotate – lift off – 170 knots, climbing out – undercarriage up. The reassuring clunks were heard as the wheel struts contacted and engaged with their locks, and the aircraft heaved almost imperceptibly as the large doors moved and closed over them. It was suddenly a lot quieter as the airframe cleaned up and the reflected ground resonance of the jet blast was left behind.

'Undercarriage up,' confirmed the co-pilot as the red indicator lights on the indicator panel extinguished and throttles were eased to 93% with 'cruise' selected. Still climbing smoothly – FL 300, throttles advanced to 95% – 12,000 feet – suddenly the peace was shattered by the sound of the cabin pressurisation warning horn, as it blasted out to signify that the cabin pressure had failed. However, no-one appeared to be concerned by this regular occurrence as all that it meant in this instance was that the aircraft was climbing faster than the cabin pressurisation could catch up! 250 knots, 20,000 feet – 300 knots – 0.86M, top of climb – level out – Cyprus here we come!

Certainly it was more comfortable when flying at altitude, as the judder and jolt of the ground beneath the wheels had given way to a gentle vertical heaving as the Vulcan occasionally rode through patches of turbulent air. If you were not used to this, it could have you clutching for a sick bag accompanied by the jeers of your companions. Fortunately the Chief had never suffered from air sickness, only sea sickness, so thank heavens he wasn't in the Navy! The requirement of being strapped in to your 'seat' could be relaxed when at altitude and you could hang your feet over the edge of the 'seat' into the bomb-aimer's well above the exit door which now formed the 'floor' of the cabin. The trouble with doing this was the temperature which, at the lowest part of the cabin, was always pretty cold while the temperature at the top of the cabin was quite comfortable. Eventually your feet became too cold and 'went to sleep' causing a certain amount of cramp and discomfort. It was at such times that the realisation dawned of being on board a warplane which was totally without the creature comforts of an airliner. The cold was hardly relieved by drawing your feet up underneath your chin again into the normal, permanent 'crash position' of the sixth and seventh seat passengers.

Of course you could walk about a bit and by slackening your parachute straps you could stand in an almost upright position. By unclipping and leaving the survival pack behind in your 'seat' position you could then, with difficulty, climb the ladder from the rear cabin that ran up between the ejector seats occupied by the captain and co-pilot. At the top of the ladder, by wedging your parachute pack on the small ledge behind, in front of the canopy jettison gun, you could stand quite comfortably on the top rung and see out of the windows. This was a poor view at its best, as even the aircrew complained about it, and there was no way that you could see any of the aircraft structure from there. This was left to the rear crew members who had no windows at all but used periscopes to see the over and undersurfaces of the bomber. (Well – they did have a sort of window, high up and round, but no-one ever used it.)

Therefore, when the restricted view became boring and one of the pilots wanted to stretch his legs he would sometimes swap places with one of the rear crew members or Crew Chiefs (they must have been masochists wanting anything to do with a sixth or seventh seat position). The rear crew member or Crew Chief would then have the pleasure of flying the bomber for a quarter of an hour or so. 'Flying' was really a misnomer as the autopilot was normally engaged and it was merely a case of monitoring that everything was proceeding well. It was hard to believe that as a child the Chief's greatest aspiration was to be a train driver! He never dreamed that one day he would be sitting, albeit briefly, at the controls of one of the mightiest warplanes ever built. This certainly broke the monotony of the trip for there were no stewardesses here or any in-flight movies to keep you interested.

Frequenting the same airways as the commercial airliners on these long distance trips as they did, it was sometimes possible to see other traffic and indeed talk to them over the radio, but usually it was just a view out of the window that was always the same. Sky, sky, sky, and more sky, and although the beauty of it never ceased to impress the Chief, eventually it became impossible to stand on the steps any longer. Dead legs together with deformed shoulders that the straps of the parachute pack were now cutting into, forced him back into the rear cabin for some exercise. It was always a good moment when the 'in flight rations' were opened up as there was usually something good in there. Although everyone had ordered what they fancied at the time, there was normally a general swap shop in operation with different fillings of sandwiches being bartered around, (two cheese sandwiches were the going rate for a leg of chicken). The coffee, tea, or fruit juice was usually served by one or other of the Crew Chiefs, who were often heard to curse as some was spilled if the aircraft hit a bumpy patch.

It was, of course, possible to get some sleep sometimes as eventually your body became accustomed to being trussed up in its emergency equipment and the monotonous whine of the intercom acted like an audible sleeping draught. Unfortunately you then awoke after an hour or so, cold, severely cramped, and wishing you hadn't bothered.

It was now time to start letting down for the SBA (Sovereign Base Area) at Akrotiri that they were heading for and all of the uneaten rations were packed away, the thermos flasks sealed and stowed, and the various items of safety equipment checked by each crew member. The non-'snatch disconnect' oxygen hose leads for the sixth and seventh seat positions were then disconnected below the height that they would be required (10,000 ft.) The descent, approach, and landing created no problems and, after the Vulcan taxied onto its allotted dispersal, the engines were shut down and the crew completed their shutdown checks with no small feelings of relief that a long and uncomfortable journey was at last over.

The door opened with a hiss and the bottom half of the ladder was slid down, enabling the two Chiefs to climb out, shrugging off their Mae Wests with sighs of relief, and then helping the rest of the crew down with all the baggage etc.

The groundcrew at most stations those days were completely un-familiar with the Vulcan bomber, being mostly overawed by its size, grace, and beauty, for it was deemed by the majority to be the sleekest shape that had ever taken to the air.

They also seemed to view the emerging crew, trailing or carrying all the trappings of flight about them, with similar awe and were only too pleased to fall over themselves to help, particularly when this involved climbing up the ladder to the cabin. It seemed that 'seeing inside the Vulcan' would earn some mysterious accolade for them. Somehow for the aircrew and Crew Chiefs there was instead almost a sense of dis-appointment. They realised all too well that a flight in a Vulcan, which many would give their right arm for, was really nothing more than a boring and uncomfortable interlude in an otherwise demanding and satisfying job.

The AAPP had been left running due to the lack of a correct ground power set, and the Chief went to get a pair of steps while his opposite number opened the bomb doors for him as the pannier would have to be removed. The crew coach had to wait whilst this was winched down as it was necessary for the aircrew to assist. The Chief unloaded his bicycle from the pannier to the laughter of the ground crew, who obviously thought it was mildly incongruous that a multi-million pound aircraft like the Vulcan should be used for a task so mundane as flying the Chief's bicycle to Cyprus!

After flight checks and refuelling were completed quickly, and after leaving instructions for the pannier to be stashed in one of the hangars, it was off in the crew coach to the various messes to book in and get a welcome shower and a meal. It was there that they were in for their first rude awakening.

Owing to the current political situation in Cyprus, resulting from the invasion and annexure of the northern half of the island by the Turkish army, all of the British civilians on the island had been drawn into the SBA (Sovereign Base Area) for safety reasons. In particular, the Sergeants' Mess was more than overflowing with personnel, as it had been designed to cater for about 200 to 300 SNCOs in total, and there were 1,500 or more people existing from it now!

That evening they pretty soon found out that socialising of any sort was very difficult, particularly in the bar. If you wanted a drink, it was necessary to get into the bar before opening time and take a tray with you! You had to buy enough drinks with your first order to last the night out as one thing was certain, you wouldn't be able to get near the bar again for the rest of the evening.

The television lounge was full to overflowing with seated and standing people everywhere, and others craning over the heads of people standing in the doorway to see a little of what was happening on screen.

A trip to the station cinema fared worse, with it being full up half an hour before the performance commenced. They were lucky I suppose, because if they had not flown in and been regarded as aircrew they probably wouldn't even have got a bed, and been required to sleep on a camp bed in some corridor or other as many of the people obviously were.

Breakfast on the next day was something to be experienced, as there were queues a mile long at the servery. It was obvious that the two Chiefs would not get food before it was time to start work again, and so they would forgo breakfast and hope that there was something laid on down at dispersal, or whichever place of work they attended. It was civilians who were causing traffic jams, being within the SBA for safety reasons and having no place of work to go to. It seemed that the RAF personnel who had to be at work on time would have to get up much earlier to get some breakfast before the rush started. They both felt that this was a poor show under the circumstances.

Some time ago the Vulcan squadrons that had then been based in Cyprus had been recalled to the UK owing to a rethink at top level regarding middle eastern strategy and therefore there was no provision at Akrotiri any more for the long term operation of Vulcans. Everything would have to be brought out from the UK and an adequate supply route established.

There were three more Vulcans arriving on the next day, complete with the aircrews, Crew Chiefs, and groundcrews via Hercules transport – hopefully with enough spares in the panniers to see them through for a while. Boy! Akrotiri was going to get a little more crowded tomorrow! The Chief could see already that his proposed three-month tour here was not going to be the picnic he thought it would be. It would certainly be a lot worse than the Sunflower that he had hoped for, or even when he was last in Cyprus as a member of the U.N. peace-keeping force 'UNFICYP' as a helicopter crewman. It seemed to him that this wonderful paradise island had been ruined forever.

He was completely right of course, as over the next few days things became very fraught indeed and the practice low-level bombing sorties, being flown out along the Italian low-level route, were not going as planned either.

The exercises involved staging through Malta three times each day, once in the morning to drop off the Crew Chief, once midday for fuel etc. and once in the evening to pick up the Crew Chief again. This was necessary because Crew Chiefs were not allowed to fly on low-level sorties due to the extra time it would take for the rear crew to abandon the aircraft in an emergency. Because of this requirement, a bombing sortie was missed each day and there was much discussion about it at squadron planning level. It was even mooted that a seven-day week would have to be worked by everyone to meet the training requirement.

It was then that the Chief came up with a good idea to solve this crisis, which would at the same time get him out of this hell hole and to the more civilised environment of Malta for the duration!

He suggested to the wing commander that it would be a good idea to take a Crew Chief to Malta, drop him off with a pannier full of spares, and leave him there for the duration of his tour to look after the Vulcans staging through. This would mean two fewer landings each day, less expenditure of airframe hours and fatigue life which was critical, and more low-level runs over the Italian route. The idea went down very well indeed, as he knew it would, and he was very surprised that the wing commander didn't rumble that it was proposed more for selfish reasons than operational efficiency for his reaction was, 'Yes . . . great idea Chief, but who in their right mind would volunteer for a job like that?'

It was obvious to the Chief that the Officers' Mess was not as crowded as the Sergeants' Mess!

'Well . . . I wouldn't mind giving it a go,' replied the Chief, with mounting apprehension that the boss had someone else in mind, 'it's a job I would like very much indeed.'

'Really?' replied the wing commander, 'well if you think you can hack it, the job's yours . . . but I want you to bear it in mind that if you find things too much, or if you get too bored in Malta all on your own, then you must signal through and I'll get you replaced right away.' The wing commander obviously thought that his luck was in, having such a willing chap readily to hand! 'When can you leave Chief?' the boss asked.

'On this morning's trip if you like! I already have my pannier packed,' replied the Chief, thinking how fortuitous it was that he hadn't, apart from his bicycle, unpacked the pannier he had brought along – the Sunflower packup he had assembled would be just the job for this little jaunt.

It would, of course, mean that they had to land at Malta on the way out to offload the Crew Chief and the pannier. This would be slung as usual in the bomb bay, but they could still get three runs over the low-level route, which was almost as good.

'OK Chief,' said the wing commander with a beam on his face, 'get your kit together, and I'll square it with everyone.'

The Chief couldn't believe that his idea had been so readily accepted and made his way to the Mess to pick up his kit – before anyone changed their minds.

CHAPTER 8

AN EXCURSION TO MALTA

Even in January 1975 the warm and welcoming air of Malta felt somehow good after the oppressive and threatening atmosphere in Cyprus, as the Chief climbed down the ladder of his Vulcan, which had just taxied in and parked on the TASF (Transit Servicing Aircraft Flight) dispersal at Luqa.

His departure from Akrotiri had been so swift that he had not found the time to say goodbye or offer any explanations to his friends for his going, but they would find out soon enough, he thought with a wry smile. Perhaps they would also envy him a little as they had not had the foresight to make a getaway from the man-made hell which the overcrowded environment of the SBA (Sovereign Base Area) at Akrotiri could certainly be described as.

The Chief requested a bowser to top-up the Vulcan's fuel as he busied himself with the turnaround servicing on his bomber. This was not XM651 but another aircraft entirely, from 44 Squadron, as it was this unit that had been selected for the Cyprus detachment and all accompanying aircraft had been brought under their banner. The Crew Chiefs were also in a pool at Akrotiri, but from now on his role would be a very different one as he busied himself with the reception, turnarounds, and servicing of transitory Vulcans, all on his own, for the next three months.

He had already found willing help on his first day, as locally enlisted Maltese airmen from TASF swarmed around the Vulcan eager to lend a hand. It seemed that all the Chief really had to do during his stay was supervise refuelling, sign up paperwork, strap in crews and expedite departures. When this turnaround had been completed it would be time to formulate his plan of action to bring a semblance of order into the rest of his stay.

The existing Maltese set-up appeared to be that his aircraft were to be handled by TASF, referred to locally as 'Tassaff', whose job it was to handle all visiting aircraft. They believed that this was their job alone as visiting aircraft did not normally carry a Crew Chief, in fact they had very little notion of what a Crew Chief was or what he did for a living. The Chief was glad about this for, had they known, it would have been all too easy for them to take the easy option and let him get on with it!

The pannier, which had been offloaded by the aircrew whilst the turnaround was being carried out, was stored temporarily for that night in one of the TASF ground equipment garages. As it was Wednesday, there would be Vulcans passing through the next day and then no more until the following Monday, which would give the Chief plenty of time to set up his local 'empire' and establish his local contacts. He had always believed that the establishment of friendly relations with local service departments paid dividends. When you were in difficulties at any time, there was always someone who was willing to help out a mate, whereas sometimes it was very difficult to get any help at all if an 'us and them' situation was allowed to develop.

There was a top dispersal pan complete with Nissen hut that was near to the TASF buildings and the Chief found this to be unoccupied so he went to have a look. It would be ideal, he thought, for the establishment of his 'empire' and so, after undertaking negotiations with the engineering officer at TASF, he was able to claim it as his own and planned to get his pannier moved there as soon as possible.

After these initial negotiations were complete, the Chief retired to the TASF coffee bar, where he made acquaintance with the engineering tradesmen and learned that there was a big exercise coming through on the day after tomorrow, which was a Saturday. Everyone was unhappy as this entailed working for the best part of the weekend.

Not being one to miss out on excitement, and having nothing better to do after he had dealt with the last Vulcan until Monday, the Chief volunteered his services to help out and this was more than gratefully accepted.

He then passed a very productive weekend marshalling around Buccaneers (Navy jobs) and Lightnings (Fright'nins), together with the occasional Canberra. He involved himself in refuelling and towing, much to the delight of the TASF personnel who were a really friendly bunch and now accepted this strange 'Crew Chief' as one of their own.

There was even a barbecue at the TASF flight sergeant's house (he was a locally enlisted Maltese SNCO) to celebrate the end of the weekend's exercise, to which the Chief was cordially invited.

Monday dawned, and the Chief was up and about early. He had to let ATC (Air Traffic Control) know how he would like the arrivals and departures of the Vulcans to be handled, ensuring they were to use the top dispersal by the Nissen hut that he had now occupied and had 'officially' entitled 'Vulcan Dispersal'. ATC were not to know that he had made all these arrangements himself and from their high level of co-operation it was obvious that they would fall over themselves to help what they obviously saw as a status symbol for their station – active Vulcan bombing operations! ATC at Luqa was a civilian organisation, likewise the fire service, for the airfield doubled as the civilian airport on the island. This, for most service people who did not like dealing with 'civvies', was a stumbling block but the Chief never found it so.

He ascertained that his first Vulcan would be coming in at 12.30 and so, after making a mental note of what he would like to beg, borrow or steal to furnish the 'Vulcan dispersal', he departed for TASF to get a coffee.

On arrival, he was greeted like a long lost friend. When he 'mentioned' that he had a Vulcan coming in at 12.30 the duty controller wrote it up on his board muttering, 'They omitted to tell me that,' and he detailed some handlers to see it in and complete the turn-around servicing. The Chief could hardly believe his ears, as TASF appeared to be only too willing to take on the hard work for him and he certainly had no intention of telling them otherwise. It seemed that they were so grateful that he had turned out to help them over the weekend, nothing was too much trouble in return! This could turn out to be a very pleasant three-month detachment indeed!

The Vulcan duly arrived, and was turned around by the Maltese airmen for the next sortie, where it was planned to 'have a bash' at the Italian route, then return to Malta for more fuel and a further turn-around servicing. Another go at the Italian route was then planned, and finally – off 'home' to Akrotiri.

Everything went well and the Vulcan departed leaving the Chief to install a desk, which had magically appeared, in his dispersal hut and a couple of chairs that the lads at TASF had found were going spare – things were looking better already!

The next priority was a telephone, and the Chief felt that he would have to play this one a little cool. He knew that if he asked for a telephone to be installed, as his occupation of the premises was unofficial he would never get one. He had to make this sound official and imply that the fact he did not have a phone was a major cock up for which heads would roll. He contacted the PBX (another civilian-manned post) and, in a terribly officious manner, asked when the phone for the Vulcan detachment was going to be installed. He went on to say that he had expected it on Friday, it didn't arrive and this was a pretty bad show, especially as the Vulcan detachment was supposed to be a priority that rated co-operation as a full 'operational necessity'. 'You'll hang yourself one day!', the Chief thought as the PBX got themselves all worked up because no-one had told them. They would give it their immediate and urgent attention. They would also find out who was responsible and discipline him! Half an hour later the phone was installed.

'Another little problem solved,' thought the Chief, as he surveyed his ever growing inventory. 'I could do with some shelves,' he thought, which would get the spares out of the pannier and into some decent looking storage – that would be a job for another day though.

His Vulcan had landed, in the meantime, after its first sortie of the day and arrived on dispersal for turnaround. The Chief commenced the refuelling operation as the Maltese airmen swarmed over the bomber topping up the rapid airs and the nitrogen storage bottles for various systems such as H2S and door closing.

They wanted 80% fuel this time, which the Chief dialled up on the control panel in the port undercarriage bay, and he climbed into the cockpit to monitor the C of G meter while the fuel was pumped in. The front tanks filled right up, the Chief noticed; that wasn't right, they should have gone through at 80%. He climbed out and stopped the refuelling operation while he checked out the fuses for the tank transfer valves. Finding nothing amiss, he climbed back in and, using the fuel pumps, transferred fuel from the forward number one tanks to the number two tanks, to bring the forward tanks down to 80%. Refuelling was again commenced, and the same thing happened with the next tanks in line – they over-filled. 'Damn good start to the detachment,' thought the Chief, as he climbed out once more to stop the refuelling and unhook the tanker, which he sent away, as this was going to take him some time to sort out.

He had a good idea that the fault would lie in the relay banks, situated in the refuelling control panels in the port and starboard undercarriage bays. These were notorious for causing trouble, so he got a pair of steps and climbed up to the panel in the port bay.

On removing the cover, which was held in place by four 'dzus' fasteners, he could see immediately that one of the wires was off a relay coil, which would mean that the panel had to be removed and serviced in a bay. The ruling was that if one of these panels failed for any reason it had, without default, to be bay serviced before it was refitted.

Now the Chief knew that there wasn't a bay at Luqa with the facilities to do this and only he knew that this was a mandatory requirement, which he certainly could circumnavigate.

He duly removed the panel and took it into the TASF stores, where the storeman looked on wide-eyed, as the Chief began to test the security of all the wires in the loom, finding out to his dismay that a quantity of them were almost corroded off. There was only one thing for it so, with a roll of 'uni-nyvin' cable and a trusty soldering iron, he set to work to partially rewire the panel.

This was a nine-hour job, or even more, so the final sortie for that day was postponed and he left the aircrew to make all the arrangements to take off for Akrotiri on the next morning.

He was about halfway through the job when word of what was going on must have spread about, as the junior engineering officer from TASF came in to see for himself. The J. Eng. O. knew that what the Chief was doing was against the rule book and the discussion became quite heated, as the J. Eng. O. tried to pull rank and have the Vulcan grounded until a suitable spare panel could be flown out from Akrotiri. This didn't go down well with the Chief, who didn't fancy any such delay being put down to him, and the J. Eng. O. eventually left, muttering that he was going to take this little matter higher up the chain of command.

The Chief carried on with his tedious job and, on completion, refitted the panel to the Vulcan and checked it out, to find that it was now completely serviceable. He called up the refuelling tanker again and the refuelling operation was completed in good time. Of course, the paperwork had to be completed for the job and it was here that the role of the Crew Chief became fully effective. What he did was to complete a job card saying that temporary repairs had been carried out to a refuelling panel and then a 'green line' entry was made in the F700 to the effect that the aircraft was declared 'fit to fly' for one trip only (back to Akrotiri). There the panel would have to be removed and bay checked. 'That'll be one in the eye for the TASF Eng. O.,' thought the Chief, who knew that the TASF Eng. O. was blissfully unaware that the Chief was authorised to do this.

The aircrew had arrived and were 'crewing in', when the TASF Jnr. Eng. O. arrived in a Land Rover, complete with the senior engineering officer, a wing commander. The wing commander, full of his own importance, got out and strode forward to the Chief saying, 'This aeroplane isn't going anywhere Chief, you had better get the crew out . . . now!'

The Chief explained the situation to the captain over his intercom who decided to leave all systems running whilst the situation was sorted out as he too knew that he was going back to Akrotiri in spite of what would transpire in the next few minutes.

The steps clanked as the captain descended and he went into the dispersal hut with the engineering officers. The Chief never did find out what transpired inside the hut, but very soon the two engineering officers came out with faces like thunder and the smiling captain climbed back into his waiting Vulcan, finished his checks, and departed.

The Chief never heard another thing about this incident for the rest of his stay and after that was left very much to his own devices with no interference whatsoever from the local engineering hierarchy. The level of co-operation from TASF actually improved, if that was at all possible, as the 'prestige' of Vulcan operations was, in their eyes, elevated to a higher plateau by the authority that appeared to be vested solely in the Crew Chief.

The next day dawned with a clear blue sky and, once again, a Vulcan was expected in at 11.30 hours, and again at 15.00 hours, and the day passed uneventfully, as the Chief managed to get some sunbathing hours in at the dispersal whilst his Vulcan was away flying.

The weekend soon arrived and the chief took good advantage of his free time, and took the first of what would prove to be many trips on the island buses to explore every corner of this very pleasant island. The island buses are something to behold, as each one appears to be the pride and joy of its owner, being fitted out with its own shrine at the front end. They certainly make a very expedient and colourful way of exploring the island. Saturday morning was passed at the 'Blue Grotto', a rock formation on the coast where you can take boat trips through a large natural rock arch formation connected to the cliffs, and, in the afternoon, time was spent watching the local sub-aqua club engaged in diving nearby. Saturday evening was usually spent in the bar of the Sergeants' Mess, where he had made acquaintance with many of the locals, and on Sunday he usually lay in bed until about midday, when he would rise and decide what was to be done in the afternoon. This was the life! He could but only imagine the hardships back at Akrotiri, and they thought that he had drawn the short straw!

The following week his first Vulcan came through on the Tuesday, and he turned it around as normal in late morning, and then went for dinner before it returned for yet another turnaround servicing.

The Chief had no sooner sat down to his meal however, when the phone in the kitchen rang with a message for him – his aircraft had a problem, and was returning to Luqa for an emergency landing. The Chief rushed from the Mess and leapt aboard his bike, arriving back at the dispersal at the same time as the junior engineering officer from TASF. The J. Eng. O. told him that his Vulcan had run into bad weather and suffered a lightning strike that had caused no apparent structural damage, but the compasses were suspect and so they were being talked home by ATC.

The Chief realised that he now had before him a very big task before his Vulcan would fly again. 'Eyeballs in the sky' eventually denoted that his aircraft was on finals and it landed without incident, but was pursued by fire tenders during its last few hundred yards of runway before coming to a halt and shutting down on the threshold. It was met there by the Chief and a tug with towing team, who quickly removed it to the Vulcan dispersal.

The 'debrief' from the crew was quite an eye-opener, as the lightning had hit fair and square, with the whole aircraft being lit up with an eerie glow for seconds afterwards, and all of the instruments went temporarily crazy. All except the compasses recovered thereafter.

The TASF handlers were completing the turnaround servicing as the Chief got back out to his aircraft, first of all to start checking the structure. Fortunately nothing of note was found, except for some slight burn marks on several dielectric aerial panels, which were exit marks, and it was found that the Collins VHF transmitter was also unserviceable, so this was changed.

The biggest job, of course, was to check the integrity of the earth bonding between components and the structure, and between various parts of the structure itself. This actually took the Chief two long days of de-panelling, and crawling about the outside and inside of the airframe, but all appeared to be sound in this department. It would have been a different story, however, had the Vulcan been on the ground at the time, as he vividly remembered an aircraft back at Waddington that had been struck by lightning on a dispersal overnight. The whole fin had been split open as if with a can opener as the heavy voltage from the lightning found its way to earth through the structure and the conductive tyres. The earth-bonding lead to the dispersal plinth had been vapourised and none of the metal core was to be seen, just a blackened line of carbonised rubber across the concrete!

The Chief then had the most difficult part of the task in front of him, as the compass amplifiers proved to be useless and had to be changed. This was to be followed by a compass swing and time was now pressing, as there was considerable pressure being put on him, from Akrotiri, to complete the job as soon as possible.

To compass swing a Vulcan was no mean task, as a 'Watts datum compass' was required, together with the datum poles which had to be screwed into fitments underneath the Vulcan. Weather conditions also had to be just right, as the wind speed had to be below a certain figure, not gusting, and the humidity had to be within certain limits. Guess what? The weather had now taken a turn for the worse, and Malta was experiencing the worst fortnight of weather for many years. Torrential rain was experienced, together with high winds, and compass swinging looked like an impossible task.

Problem number one reared its ugly head, and that was the Watts datum compass. For some obscure reason nobody could find the one belonging the Nimrod Squadron that was operating from Malta, and the datum rods would also not fit! Akrotiri was signalled, and while they could get a Watts datum compass flown over, all wands were back in the UK . . . someone had forgotten to pack them in the panic that had ensued to get four Vulcans out to Cyprus in double quick time . . . not to worry . . . he would improvise!

The Chief went to the station workshops and had two steel rods welded onto steel bolts that could be screwed into the fitments under the Vulcan, and these were in turn banded in self-adhesive Day-Glo.

The Watts datum compass arrived the next morning on board a 'Belfast', and the Vulcan, together with all the equipment and a sceptical navigator, was transported to the compass-swing dispersal on a remote part of the airfield.

The procedure adopted during compass swinging was that the wands were screwed into the sockets provided in the aircraft structure underneath and the aircraft was towed carefully to a known heading, using the on-board compass, and halted. Being non-standard wands, these were then bent, using a spirit level, into the vertical position and sighted up by the navigator who was positioned about fifty yards to the rear to sight up the wands with his compass. The problems were too evident, for the wands were waving and vibrating in the high wind and, as it was also raining, the poor old navigator was enshrouded, together with his compass mounted on a tripod, under an enormous plastic bag.

Somehow though, in spite of all the adverse conditions, the sightings were all taken, the corrections made and the Vulcan was made ready to return to Akrotiri.

As a precaution, the compass swing was repeated after it arrived at its destination, and – guess what? – there were no further corrections to be made. The Chief felt that they had all achieved the near impossible under what seemed like totally unsuitable conditions.

The next day saw one of the Vulcans suffer a bird strike in the port engine whilst coming in to land. An unfortunate seagull had been ingested, fortunately during landing when the engines were at low power, and after inspection of the engine, it was found that no damage had ensued and the seagull had gone through with little or no effect.

It was a very unpleasant job inspecting an engine after such an event, as a seagull, being a scavenger, did not smell very pleasant when it was spread about the insides of an axial-flow compressor!

The weeks passed and the weather improved, and the Chief's knowledge of the island improved as the time passed, and there were many interludes of Vulcan unserviceability to cope with in between.

One incident involved an engine which refused to start because the 'cracker box', which provided the ignition sequence, refused to function. This could have proved a distinct inconvenience, as these were in short supply and there were not enough to equip all spares packups with one. With typical ingenuity however, the Chief raided the Luqa stores and found that the Canberra unit had almost the same timing sequence, so one of these was fitted, functioned perfectly and was green lined for the return flight to Akrotiri. How they managed to sort out the paperwork eventually for these units heaven only knows!

The day eventually arrived when the Chief's tour of duty came to an end in Malta, and it was arranged that he would fly back to the UK on a Belfast transport aircraft that was due to leave shortly after his Vulcan was seen off.

Preparatory to this, a transitory Vulcan from Scampton passed through and the Chief saw this as a golden opportunity to send his flying and survival kit home. This would save lugging it across country from Brize Norton, where the Belfast would be landing, to Waddington, which was his eventual destination.

The Crew Chief on board the Scampton Vulcan was an old friend of his, Clive Penton. They had served together on Argosy transports at Benson in Oxfordshire for a number of years. His friend was only too pleased to help out and so the cumbersome kit was stored on board the Scampton Vulcan for transit back to the UK . . . 'One problem out of the way,' thought the Chief.

The next day his Vulcan arrived, and he met it with all his personal kit packed ready to climb into the Belfast after he had turned it around and it had departed. Everything went smoothly up to engine start.

'Clear one?' queried the Captain to which the Chief responded, 'Clear one', and the Palouste hose stiffened as air was delivered to the starter motor. The engine motored over smoothly and lit with the characteristic rumbling howl, which rose in crescendo as the throttle was advanced to idle. 'Clear two,' from the captain was responded to in turn by, 'Clear two,' from the Crew Chief. The Palouste hose once again stiffened as air was delivered to the starter turbine, but there was no response from the engine. 'Two's not turning Chief,' reported the captain, and the Chief moved to the number two starter exhaust, where it was obvious that air was passing through, but there was no transmission of movement to the engine.

Number one was accordingly shut down, and the crew disembarked whilst the Chief investigated the fault.

After crawling down the intake and rotating the engine, it was obvious that the fault must lie in the starter, which meant that this would have to be removed. 'Damn!' he cursed, for he knew now that the Belfast would have to go without him. 'Never mind,' he thought, 'there'll be another one soon, so I'll fix this job and get away tomorrow hopefully'. He was secure in this knowledge, for he just happened to have a spare starter in his spares packup.

The engine panels under number two were lowered to gain access to the starter and the Chief then looked up in dismay. The starter had obviously been assembled to the engine in the engine service bay, before the engine had been fitted. The clown that had fitted it had done so with the 'King clamp' holding it fitted 180° out of position. This meant that, while it could be assembled to the engine and also dismounted while the engine was out of the aircraft, there was no way that it could be done with the engine in situ! The problem was now compounding itself.

There was no other option than to drop the engine, which the Chief would certainly not be able to do by himself, and this meant sending an engine change team all the way from Akrotiri to carry out this task.

The engine-change team arrived the next day complete with all their equipment and straight away ploughed in with a will to remove the engine. In charge of the engine change team was a small Scottish sergeant, who drove his men unmercifully, but with such a sense of humour and unfailing wit, that they scarcely knew that they were being whipped.

The engine was out in about three hours and the offending starter motor was removed, and just as it was laid on its side by the engine, a small octagonal brass pipe just fell out of it with a tinkle onto the concrete apron. The small turbine was rotated and found to be free, so obviously this small piece of brass had been jamming it. There was no damage and, by examining the replacement starter motor, it was determined that the offending pipe was merely a small pressure-sensing pipe which was mounted in the driving airflow. It was refitted using 'Loctite' to ensure it stayed where it should and a signal was sent to Akrotiri explaining matters. A long argument ensued over the airwaves about possible damage caused to the starter motor and whether or not it could be used. However, as it was now refitted and the engine almost reinstalled, there was no way the team would willingly take it all out again to put another starter on the aircraft!

It was obvious to those in Malta that the pipe had vibrated out whilst the aircraft was in flight and dropped into the turbine, jamming it and preventing movement. If it had gone in whilst the turbine was rotating at speed . . . it would have been goodbye turbine! The Akrotiri authorities then took some convincing, but the Chief managed it and authorisation was granted for one flight only with the starter on a red-line entry for inspection at destination. By this time the destination had been changed to the UK as it had been decided to return this aircraft for a scheduled check servicing. The Chief had instructions to accompany it to the UK on completion of rectification.

By now the engine was fully installed and ready for runs which, as it was now 21.00 hours, they decided to carry out the next morning.

The next day they arose early and ordered a tug to position the Vulcan on the engine-running pan, which when they arrived, they found to be nothing more than a smallish concrete apron with a blast wall made up to about two feet high behind. When the Vulcan was positioned on this, the jet pipes were five feet above the top of the blast wall and hanging over it!

The engine sergeant decided that they couldn't possibly run in that position and he moved the bomber about thirty feet forward so that, at least, the blast would be deflected by the wall and not cause any damage to the airfield surface, and they prepared to start the engines.

They were just about to wind up the number two engine, when up rolled a Land Rover from ATC. 'You can't run it here,' said the guy behind the wheel, 'you must position it correctly on the concrete apron!'

A few words of explanation were offered by the engine sergeant, but to no avail – ATC knew where the Vulcan had to be and it couldn't be run unless it was positioned to their satisfaction. Humour was sadly lacking thereafter as they ordered up a tug again, attached the towing bar and repositioned the aircraft.

The engine sergeant then climbed into the cockpit preparatory to starting the engine with a glint in his eyes, muttering something about, 'I'll bloody well show 'em.'

The Chief went on line outside and realised with a wry smile that the engine sergeant was going to run all four engines, and not just number two to prove the starter. Sure enough, as soon as all the pre-start checks had been carried out, 'Clear one,' came the request over the intercom. 'Clear one,' responded the Chief, still grinning, as the air hose from the Palouste stiffened, passing air to number one starter. Soon all four engines were running and the Chief could see that the exhaust, even at a low power setting, was missing the blast wall completely and flattening the grass behind for some distance.

'Clear to 60%,' came the request from the cockpit. 'Clear 60%,' responded the Chief, and the engine note changed to a dull roar that shook the ground as four Olympus 301s rotated up to 60% power setting. The grass stood this well, the Chief noted, with only a few sods and small stones taking to the air and soon the throttles were back at idle with the four twin-spool turbines whining lazily.

'Got to do a slam check now Chief,' said the voice over the intercom, 'Keep a weather eye out.'

'OK to slam check,' responded the Chief, and with that the engine sergeant rapidly pushed the throttles hard forward against the stops. With a tortured roar the four engines wound up to maximum power, deafening the Chief even through his protective headset. The Vulcan's nose dipped and the airframe strained like a racehorse on the leash as the searing 80,000 lb. of exhaust blast lifted the grass to the rear like a giant roll of turf. It exploded into a flying mass of grass, stones and earth that tumbled rapidly across the airfield in the direction of the main runway.

After a few seconds of this, throttles were eased back to idle with the Vulcan's nose easing up as it once again settled to a less strained position on the apron. As the dust and mayhem slowly cleared behind the aircraft the Chief could see that there had been a hole excavated about 100-foot long, forty feet at its widest, and up to four or six inches deep in places. The debris was spread far and wide across the airfield including a substantial part of the main runway!

It didn't take very long for the ATC Land Rover to return with a now very flustered official who looked decidedly embarrassed. The engine sergeant climbed out of the cockpit, looked at him with a satisfied look on his face and without a word spread his hands in a manner that said, 'I told you so!'

The result of this escapade was that the airfield was shut down for two hours and civilian air traffic diverted elsewhere in the Med. while a major cleanup operation was initiated.

From the groundcrew's viewpoint the engine runs had proved satisfactory, and all that was necessary was to inform the aircrew, who then made plans to return to UK the following day with the Chief accompanying them. 'This should be fun,' he mused, 'I've got to fly with them, and my flying kit is in Scampton! Not to worry,' he thought, 'I'll bluff my way through this one somehow.'

The next day dawned, and the Chief was up early to prepare his Vulcan and stow the luggage and duty frees, and by the planned crew-in time he had everything completed and was drinking a coffee in the TASF crew room when the aircrew arrived.

The crew-in and start up progressed as normal and, after the engines were burning and turning with clearance to taxi obtained from ATC, the Chief climbed aboard, stowed the ladder, closed the door and strapped himself into the confines of the sixth seat position. The rear crew members were far too busy to notice he was in his normal working uniform with no flying kit at all.

Taxi and takeoff went as planned, and pretty soon they were levelled off and flying in their assigned air corridor on the way home. The Chief unstrapped and climbed the ladder in between the captain and co-pilot's ejector seats. The Captain turned to speak, noticing at the same time the lack of any flying kit about the Chief.

'Hello Chief, where's your flying suit and bonedome?' asked the captain in a surprised manner.

'In Scampton,' replied the Chief. Upon looking further the captain then asked, 'I suppose your parachute and headset are there as well?' 'Yep,' replied the Chief as the captain resignedly looked to heaven. 'Ah well, if we have to bale out, you'll just have to hang onto the AEO and hope for the best,' he eventually said with a wry grin and nothing more was mentioned about the matter for the rest of the flight.

The letdown for Waddington commenced and the crew began to stow their non-essential items of equipment preparatory to approach and landing. The AEO reported that the weather at Waddington was a bit 'iffy'. This was unusual, for Waddington was a master diversion airfield with weather that was reputedly always good or at least never below the minimum requirements for flying.

'We'll go in for a look-see and try to get down,' the captain decided. They actually made three attempts but did not break through the cloudbase, into the rain that was falling heavily below, before the cut-off height was reached, and to cap it all there was a crosswind as well. On the final attempt they were just about to call it off, when suddenly the aircraft bucked violently, just as if it had touched the ground, and then gave several smaller oscillations before settling down. They were at about 250 feet altitude on the approach at the time.

'What the hell was that?' asked the navigator, looking around to see that all was well and noting the very startled faces of the other crew members. 'I reckon that was a near air miss,' said the captain. 'Whatever it was must be in some real trouble now, I would think . . . that settles it, we're diverting to Cottesmore.'

The captain eased the throttles forward, selected air brakes in and undercarriage up, at the same time informing Waddington tower that

50S/201/1/P3

OC Eng Wg

EXERCISE FOREARM DETACHMENT - CHF TECH J B GOODWIN - ASC

1.   One of the main features of No 50 Squadron's recent Exercise Forearm detachment to Cyprus was the excellent training value provided by the Sicilian and Calabrian low level routes on our 'Italian Rangers'.   Throughout the detachment we flew 2 X 3 day Italian rangers per week - each scheduled to provide 3 sorties.   The original 1 Gp plan had been to fly an ASC into Luqa on the Monday inbound Vulcan and retrieve him on the Friday outbound Vulcan.   However, because of the HQ 1 Gp ruling which precluded low level while carrying an ASC in these circumstances, this would have resulted in 2 relatively wasteful high level only transit flights each week.   To obviate this, Chief Technician J B Goodwin - one of the 5 ASC's on the detachment - volunteered to travel to Luqa (on a 46 Gp scheduled aircraft) and remain there throughout the detachment (a period of 5 weeks) as our 'resident Vulcan ASC'.

2.   In the normal course of events, therefore, Goodwin - with limited assistance from the Vulcan aircrews and/or Luqa's Transit Aircraft Servicing Flight (depending upon the workload involved)was instrumental in generating launching and recovering 4 sorties per week out of the nominal total of 10 sorties per week for which the Forearm detachment was established.   In itself this was an excellent achievement from the detachment manpower point of view - providing a very cheap method of generating sorties.

3.   In the event, an excessive G count following sudden severe turbulence at Low Level, a lightning strike and the failure of an engine starter at various times during the detachment all contrived to generate an even higher workload for Goodwin. Although he had been briefed to call for manpower from the main detachment at Akrotiri should he need it at any time, Goodwin contended with all the problems (apart from an engine drop - for which his team was provided from Akrotiri) from his own resources.

4.   Each of the 50 Squadron captains - on returning from their Italian Rangers - commented in the most glowing terms on the assistance they had received from Goodwin and on the excellent job he was doing.   The attached 'testimonials' reflect the admiration and high regard which his work and efforts generated.

5.   In brief, Goodwin displayed determination, initiative, resourcefulness and organising ability of the highest order, throughout the Forearm detachment.   These qualities coupled with his enthusiasm and unfailing good humour, certainly auger well for his future career.   I should be most grateful if wou would convey our thanks to Chief Technician Goodwin but, more particularly, if you could ensure that his most commendable performance does not go unrecorded or unrewarded.

A PARKES
Wg Cdr
OC 50 Sqn

11 Mar 75

A letter of commendation from the Squadron C.O. after the Chief's efforts in Malta on exercise 'Forearm'.

we were overshooting and on our way to Cottesmore. He also informed them about the 'air miss', thanked them for their assistance, and the Vulcan climbed away; half an hour later it touched down in clear weather, safely, at Cottesmore.

The Chief quickly after-flighted the Vulcan and departed with the now disgruntled crew for the aircrew diner, for a very welcome post-flight meal. Shortly thereafter a coach arrived and conveyed them all back to Waddington.

The next day dawned bright and clear, and the Chief arrived at the squadron line buildings early to find that everyone considered he had had such a raw deal that another Chief had been despatched with a fresh crew earlier to Cottesmore to bring his Vulcan back! 'Will they be pleased when they see I have red-lined the engine for one flight to the UK!' thought the Chief, and he wondered just what the reaction would be when they read it in the Form 700. The problem would be that the Chief had completed that red-line entry, in Malta, when authorised to do so through operational necessity, and it was not permissible for the other Chief at Cottesmore to do this for another flight at 'home base'.

About an hour later, the phone rang and, sure enough, it was the broad Welsh accent of the relief Crew Chief at Cottesmore on the other end of the line wanting to know just what the hell was going on. Now the Chief felt that he really was home – in the land of rules and red tape once again. Taffy on the other end of the line wasn't best pleased, the Chief could sense, as he had to hold the phone away from his ear to avoid being deafened by the torrent of invective. However, everything was eventually sorted out with the S. Eng. O. at Cottesmore red-lining the starter again for a single ferry trip back to Waddington where it was inspected by the engine boffins and passed as serviceable. Hey ho! What a pleasant day!

CHAPTER 9

THE END OF AN ERA

The Chief's last year of service with 101 Squadron was spent as the line servicing controller, a job that he had occasionally covered in the past when the regular controller was on leave, and he now found himself carrying this out full time. His friend, the flight sergeant controller, had been promoted to warrant officer, and had moved to IX Squadron leaving the post vacant. The incoming flight sergeant was unfamiliar with the Vulcan and its operation, and so the Chief had been moved into the hot seat – a job he came to enjoy.

His friend, the 101 squadron warrant officer, had also reached the end of his service, and had been 'dined out' in a fitting manner at the Sergeants' Mess as he retired to civilian life. His final departure had been noteworthy, as he was towed around the station and out of the main gate in a model Vulcan by the squadron groundcrew members; this accolade was normally reserved for retiring station commanders.

Unfortunately for this story, the line controller's job was very routine, and the Chief settled down to a more or less sedentary existence, controlling the workload and allocation of aircraft to various tasks from day to day. Unbeknown to him at the time, this was preparing him for the tasks that lay ahead, for promotion was very much in the offing, although at this stage he didn't have an inkling.

One day he arrived at work to find that he had been detailed for an interview with the 101 squadron senior engineer. Wondering what misdemeanours he had committed, he was full of apprehension as he walked through the door of the senior engineer's office and was motioned to a seat. After an initial exchange of pleasantries, the Chief was informed that his promotion to the rank of flight sergeant had come through, and had been approved. He was also told that, after the promotion was effective, he would be posted from Waddington to take up new duties at another station as was normal in such cases. Crew Chiefs were always high on the promotion ladder because of the multiple trade training they had undergone and the vast practical experience of aircraft type that they had amassed. However, his immediate thoughts were that he should turn down this promotion. He was on a 'last tour of duty' posting that meant he would be remaining at Waddington, he had purchased a house locally, and he was intending to spend the last three years of his twenty-two-year engagement there. Much discussion ensued and the senior engineer was very loath to accept the Chief's refusal of this promotion. Therefore he was advised to go away and think about it overnight, coming back with his final decision on the following day.

Thus, having more time to think about it and to discuss the implications with his family and friends, he became more fixed in his intention to turn it down. The rise in pay was only a matter of £5.00 per week (not too bad in those days), but, if posted away, he would spend this, and more, on travelling back and forth at weekends. Not only that, it would mean that he would have to invest in another car, as the Mk IV Zodiac that he owned at present was not up to regular long distance travelling without a lot of work being carried out. The next day he went back to see the senior engineer and informed him of his choice, also his reasons for it. He returned to the control desk and surveyed the day's tasks ahead, feeling that he had made the right decision.

Two days went by, and he was again summoned into the senior engineer's office, to be asked, 'If you were given an internal posting at Waddington rather than a posting away from the station, would you accept the promotion then?' They wouldn't tell him to where the move was and later he realised that this should have rung warning bells. The Chief thought but briefly about this new offer and decided to accept – after all, what harm could it do. He would remain at Waddington, have a 5% rise in pay, and still be associated with his beloved Vulcans. Later on, he wished he had insisted on knowing where the posting was to be before accepting it!

He found that he was to immediately take over one of the engineering shifts at IX Squadron, who operated from 'Bravo' dispersal, the former 'punishment' end of the airfield, ever since their return from Cyprus some time earlier. IX Squadron had a long and distinguished service history, but currently appeared to be undergoing a somewhat transitory period, and their reputation amongst the groundcrew at Waddington was not very good, in fact you might even say that it had hit an extremely low period.

IX Squadron had arrived back in the UK, from Akrotiri in Cyprus, as a squadron of aircraft and aircrew, with very few groundcrew. While a number of tradesmen and supervisors were drafted in from outside, the bulk of the manpower came from the other squadrons already based at Waddington. Instead of drafting-in the required ranks and trades to fill the vacancies, 44, 50, and 101 Squadrons had been asked to supply 'x' number of ranks and trades to fill the requirement. You can guess what happened – they got rid of those personnel whom they wished to be rid of for various reasons, leaving IX Squadron with an engineering nightmare. To compound this, most of the personnel drafted in from outside had no Vulcan experience at all, some of these being expected to fill the vital trade manager positions.

The Chief, as a newly appointed flight sergeant, was appointed as a shift boss over this motley collection of engineering staff, and to say that his time at IX Squadron was anything other than a nightmare would be to make a gross understatement of the truth.

Fortunately, nearly all of the Crew Chiefs, on whom the smooth running of the organisation depended, were very reliable and could be trusted to carry out their jobs in an efficient manner. Unfortunately, a hardened core of the others were decidedly hostile to the squadron, to their continued association with the Vulcan, and to just about everything else that smacked of work. These particular Crew Chiefs would rather spend their time in the crew room playing cards, leaving the airmen to get on with vital servicing such as refuelling that, according to laid down practice and orders, required the Crew Chief's undivided attention. Their expertise was required out on the job where it would have eased the pressure considerably. Unfortunately, some of the good guys were responding to this peer pressure and were well on the road to adopting this unfortunate attitude.

Confrontation followed confrontation between the flight sergeant and this core of Crew Chiefs, with one Chief in particular refusing point blank to leave his game of cards and attend his aircraft to supervise refuelling. Matters finally came to a head one night in the car park, when, after a display of insubordination that the flight sergeant had never before seen the like of, this Crew Chief was placed under close arrest and escorted to the guardroom by two of the squadron's other senior NCOs. The squadron senior engineer was called out, the Crew Chief's release was effected, and he was sent home until the next day, when he came in to be interviewed by the senior engineer. A terrible furore followed at squadron engineering level, and unfortunately a lot of smoothing over was carried out, instead of the much needed disciplinary procedures being followed through. One thing became abundantly clear, and that was that the senior engineer was not going to allow his dirty washing to be aired in public.

Things improved slightly after this, as the ringleaders amongst the core of troublesome Crew Chiefs saw that they couldn't get away with what amounted to gross negligence any longer, and, overall, they were seen to be paying more attention to their responsibilities. The crew room was made virtually out of bounds to those Crew Chiefs that had ongoing work with their aircraft. The overall tension relaxed somewhat, as there was no longer any peer pressure being applied to the more conscientious members of the engineering establishment.

Unfortunately this did not improve the overall situation, where, as mentioned previously, some of the senior NCO supervisors and tradesmen had been drafted in and been expected to 'pick up the job' as they worked along. This led to many problems. A lack of basic systems knowledge meant that diagnostic skills were lacking, particularly amongst the electrical and NBS trades where most problems seemed to occur, and rectification of defects became a long and gruelling slog. Sometimes it became necessary to borrow SNCOs and tradesmen from the other squadrons' engineering staff to cope. When these personnel arrived and sorted out the problems with very little effort, this did not make the IX Squadron groundcrew feel any better about their situation. Having said this, it has also to be said that a rectification task once started was never left uncompleted, but was always finished in time to meet the sortie. This was even if parts had to be robbed from another aircraft, with work then continuing on the faulty equipment to bring up the aircraft to which the fault had been transferred. Making the sortie became the goal of every engineer, and they completed this task magnificently, most times well against all the odds. Unfortunately, it came to the point where IX Squadron's groundcrew worked the longest hours to produce what appeared to be the most meagre results on the station. It was no surprise to have to work a shift of eight hours that drifted into ten hours or even twelve. Weekends were deemed not to exist – it was just a continual round of overtime that seemed to produce results not dissimilar to the other units, who managed to achieve it during normal working hours.

The problems faced by the flight sergeant were further compounded, as whenever he came in for the night shift, it always seemed that the important aspects of his shift's evening workload had been already organised by the day shift supervisors. This included the movement of aircraft in and out of the hangar for servicing etc. The arrangements made invariably took scant regard of the lack of manpower for the expected workload, especially regarding the best time to co-ordinate the planned aircraft movements. It was always best to move all of the aircraft one after another while a tug was available and a towing team assembled, rather than spread the task out over a whole evening. The programme could then easily be disrupted by the unavailability of a tug, and the tradesmen who formed the tugging team would have to be taken off their rectification tasks yet again. This task could easily be co-ordinated with the other squadrons' own movements, but the day shift seemed to take scant regard of this. Also, it always seemed as if the seemingly insurmountable problems of the day shift had been left for the night shift to sort out, as well as their own workload. This mostly entailed some day shift workers returning to work for part of the evening as well. The flight sergeant always had to make corrections to the preconceived plan to fit it in with his own shift's workload, and inevitably this caused friction with the senior day shift managers. Fortunately, the Flight was on very good terms indeed with the staff in engineering operations, with whom he had worked on and off for a number of years. Eventually, by arrangement, they knew not to finalise any plans for the evening's aircraft movements for IX Squadron until the incoming flight sergeant had reviewed his work load, consulted with the other squadrons, and given the OK.

The day shift obviously found out about this and much acrimony ensued, but the end result was that the Flight was left to make his own arrangements in future, and this suited him and his shift down to the ground. Finally he seemed to be getting somewhere.

When it was his shift's turn to work the day shift, this also didn't pass without interference, as it appeared that others sought to continually undermine his arrangements. When it came time to knock off at five, after he had handed over to the oncoming shift boss, the senior engineer would often 'buttonhole' him. This usually followed the form of him sticking his head out of his office door as the flight sergeant went by on his way to the car park, with the request, 'Have you got a minute Flight?' The Flight would then go into his office, to be involved in discussions ranging around squadron policy about which he had no influence or responsibility. Often he would not get away until 7 or 8 p.m. His dinner would be spoiled, and his wife angry, but – what the hell – nobody at senior level seemed to care. This was certainly a very different outfit to any other that he had been associated with throughout his previous nineteen years of service.

The squadron warrant officer was somewhat of a contrast and he was a very nice chap indeed, and about the only one around (apart from the Flight) who tried to change the way things ran from the top. It was all to no avail, as the trained manpower didn't seem to be forthcoming and also entrenched attitudes are often hard to change. The Warrant was maintaining a somewhat low profile, about to be demobbed at the end of a long and distinguished RAF career. To celebrate this occasion a party was arranged by the senior engineer at his married quarter. All of the squadron engineering hierarchy, together with their wives, were invited. They all arrived around the appointed time and a somewhat lively and pleasant occasion developed. With the cares of work forgotten, the Warrant had a good send off – until 10 p.m. that was, when a very senior squadron officer arrived, with his lady, from an Officers' Mess function. The atmosphere changed abruptly from its convivial tone to a formal, stilted gathering, where everyone became immediately on their guard.

The senior squadron officer parked on the settee, next to the flight sergeant, and engaged in conversation around the workings of the squadron. The Flight was taken aback at how out of touch this person appeared to be with the problems that were rife in the squadron below him. Eventually came the long awaited question, 'Well Flight, how do you like the IX Squadron set-up compared to your previous experiences of 101 Squadron?'

Now it just so happened that the Flight, together with the junior engineering officer who was his friend as well as being his boss, and all of the others, had consumed a goodly quantity of the senior engineer's home brew. To the senior officer's question the Flight gave a full, truthful, and lengthy reply. It all came out, his views on morale, efficiency (or lack of it), working practices etc. 'Why hold back?' he thought. Everything he said was backed up by the junior engineering officer at length, and that was virtually the end of the party. The senior officer left and everyone drifted off home, feeling that there would be repercussions on the following day – how right they were.

The junior engineering officer was hauled up before the senior officer, and told that he had been disloyal in supporting the flight sergeant's views, together with a lot of other unrepeatable things. In the Flight's corner, there were no direct repercussions such as this, but the senior officer never spoke to him again as long as they both were associated with IX Squadron – ever.

After this, the senior officer, if encountering the flight sergeant, would walk around the other side of a building rather than pass and exchange salutes with him.

It was the case that, when a Vulcan landed after a sortie, the crew would come into the 'de-brief room', where all faults requiring rectification would be passed on to the trade managers who sat opposite the crew members around a table, together with the flight sergeant as debrief supervisor. When it was this senior officer's crew, exchanges between them always took place via third parties – never as direct conversation.

Holidays were a nightmare, as the Flight was a keen caravanner and liked to tour when away, with spur of the moment decisions and varied overnight stops being the essence of the holiday. Now all that had to change, for he had to provide an itinerary beforehand with times and dates, and telephone numbers in case he needed to be contacted. This took all the pleasure out of it.

Winter was a time when you had to be on your mettle, for if snow was forecast, no more than a light covering should be allowed to build up on the Vulcan's oversurfaces because of the possibility of structural damage due to its weight. Nose-leg picketing hooks had to be fitted at all times when snow was forecast, otherwise, depending on fuel load, a mere three or four inches of snow on the mainplane could sit one of the bombers on its tail.

It was the duty of the night shift, and after that, the swing shift, to make sure that mainplanes were kept clear of snow. This was usually done by throwing a piece of 1½ in. rope over the mainplane every once in a while and, whilst holding it down over the leading and trailing edges, pulling it along the mainplane to the tip, thus clearing the snow. This was a three or four man job that could quite easily be accomplished.

Not wishing to trust the groundcrew (and by implication the flight sergeant), immediately it began to snow the senior engineer would come in to work, even in the middle of the night, and make his way out along the flight line every so often for a tour of inspection. In his own words, this was 'to make sure the snow was not building up!' Sometimes he would go out ten minutes after a Crew Chief or even just after the flight sergeant had done his rounds – 'just to double check'. Nobody liked this form of interference, the supervisors had all been doing the job for years, and it led to much humour being satirised around it. One of the Crew Chiefs painted 'right' on the senior engineer's left Wellington boot and 'left' on the right one. On one occasion they really were worn as labelled, but, again, maybe it was his way of winding them up in return. They never found that out.

In the early morning, before an aircraft was to fly, the remainder of the snow and ice was cleared from the flying surfaces by the use of hot de-icing fluid from a special de-icing vehicle. This was sprayed onto the aircraft from a gantry on top of the vehicle through a spray lance operated by one of the groundcrew, while another drove the vehicle slowly around the aircraft. The heaters in the de-icing tank on each vehicle had to be plugged in twelve hours prior to use, and this was another job that, whilst being routine, was checked punctiliously by the senior engineer. All of this was far beyond his remit and was generally seen as usurping the authority of the senior NCOs on the squadron whose responsibilities these jobs really were. This was another reason for the low morale towards work that abounded with everyone from the junior engineer downwards.

One consolation indeed was that his friend, the old 101 Squadron line controller whose job he had taken up, and who, recently promoted to Warrant Officer, had been posted in as the new squadron warrant officer for IX Squadron – provided a much needed shoulder to cry on when needed.

It happened that, one day, new station orders were posted, and a general redundancy scheme was being offered to certain ranks and trades with a very attractive payment. The Flight found that he qualified and decided that he couldn't put up with yet another year of his current squadron until the end of his service, so he decided to pop in to station headquarters on his way home to apply. As he left the IX Squadron line buildings early at 4.45 p.m. that afternoon, the senior engineer poked his head out of his office and asked his usual question, 'Before you go Flight – can you spare a minute?' Knowing that this could mean hours of (to him) meaningless discussion, the Flight took great pleasure in imparting the news, 'Not tonight, sir – I'm going over to station headquarters to apply for my redundancy!' The dumbfounded senior engineer had no reply for this and the Flight was able to depart, unhindered for once, for the station head-quarters building.

Weeks went by – nothing improved, things possibly got even worse, and the flight sergeant awaited news of his redundancy. One morning, just as he was rising late (he was on the night shift that week), the tele-phone rang, and it was his friend the junior engineering officer. 'Flight, your redundancy's through. Nobody at squadron level knows but me, so if you pop over to SHQ and get your clearance card, you can be done by mid-afternoon – I'll not breathe a word over here, as I've not been "officially" informed!'

With his uniform and all the rest of his RAF paraphernalia in a suit-case, the Flight went to headquarters to collect his clearance 'blue chit', handed everything in at stores, and collected the signatures from each department on his chit to declare that he had nothing outstanding with them.

The last signature to be collected was that of IX Squadron engineer-ing administration, and he rolled into the squadron line buildings at around 4.45 p.m. in civilian clothes to collect this. The first person to greet him was his friend the squadron warrant officer. With raised eyebrows he said, 'Hello Flight, what are you doing in civvies at this time – you're on nights tonight!'

'Not any more,' replied the Flight, and, taking his blue chit out of his inside pocket, waved it for him to see. 'Just call me mister,' he said, whereupon the senior engineer shot out of his office like a scalded cat. 'What's going on – what do you mean – you're a civilian now?'

'Yes, sir, I'm afraid so,' declared the Flight, noticing his friend, the junior engineering officer smirking in the background. 'But who's going to run the shift tonight?' asked the senior engineer.

Accepting the warrant's signature onto his blue chit, the Flight replied, 'Sorry, that's not my problem any more,' as he turned on his heel and walked off to the crew room to say goodbye to his colleagues.

Thinking back on it during later months, he felt that the organisation must have suffered a mental blockage! How was it possible that an engineering shift boss on a front line RAF Squadron could be granted redundancy without any of his immediate superiors knowing about it? He would have thought that the squadron hierarchy would at least have been informed. He found this very hard to believe, but seeing the way that defence cuts had been biting into manpower over the last year or so, and allying it to other things he had noted, he wasn't really surprised.

Over the next few months, with the help of his (then) generous redundancy payment, he set up a TV business in Lincoln, and this went very well indeed, in fact twenty-two years later he has only just given this up to move on to other things. He has had no regrets about leaving the RAF. It was a time in his life that he enjoyed very much, and he felt that he would have had no hesitation in repeating it – except for the last bit, which he found to be soul destroying, as did all of his work colleagues.

Looking back also, being in business in Lincoln as he was, he often had visits from ex-colleagues. His shop sometimes resembled an RAF Waddington crew room and he was kept up to date with the happenings at his old places of work. He never saw many IX Squadron personnel except for the Crew Chiefs, it was mostly his old colleagues from 101 Squadron that visited him. What he did hear about IX Squadron, however, was that apparently it took all of six months to replace him with another flight sergeant in his vacated post.

One day, completely out of the blue, the IX Squadron senior officer with whom he had the difference of opinion (now a civilian himself) turned up in his shop with a TV for repair, and greeted him by his Christian name as if nothing untoward had happened between them. He remained a customer for several years.

His friend the IX Squadron junior engineering officer also applied for and was granted a redundancy, and they both kept in touch for a period. I think that he became a sub-postmaster with a small caravan site behind his post office.

His old friend, the 101 Squadron warrant officer, is still a friend today, and they still attend caravan rallies and holiday together.

The Falklands Crisis blew up, the Vulcans acquitted themselves well, and shortly after that the squadrons were disbanded. Some of them were briefly converted to the flight refuelling role as Vulcan K2s, and his old Vulcan, XM651, was broken up by JCBs at Waddington and he felt very sad at that.

The Flight, now a long standing 'Mr' was on hand on the Grantham Road to say goodbye to the last flying Vulcan, XH558, when it made its tour of the county, bomb doors open, and the words 'FAREWELL' written inside for all to see.

101 Squadron reformed with VC10s converted into the flight refuelling role and operated out of Brize Norton in Oxfordshire, and IX Squadron reformed with Tornados. It was only to be hoped that IX Squadron operated now under different engineering conditions, with better morale than had existed during their latter days within the V-force at Waddington.

It was truly – 'The End of an ERA'.

INDEX